Mischief From the Back Pew

MISCHIEF
FROM THE BACK PEW

by Todd and Jedd Hafer

BETHANYHOUSE

MINNEAPOLIS, MN 55438

Mischief From the Back Pew
Copyright © 2003
Todd & Jedd Hafer

Cover illustration by Jimmy Holder
Cover design by Melinda Schumacher

Chapter 11 includes content from a concert review by Todd Hafer in the
December 1995 issue of CCM *Magazine*.

Published by Bethany House Publishers
11400 Hampshire Avenue South
Bloomington, Minnesota 55438

Bethany House Publishers is a Division of
Baker Book House Company, Grand Rapids, Michigan.

Printed in the United States of America

Library of Congress Cataloging-in-Publication Data

Hafer, Todd.
    Mischief from the back pew :   and you thought you were safe in church— /
by Todd & Jedd Hafer.
        p.   cm.
    ISBN 0-7642-2800-5
    1. Christianity—Humor.   I. Hafer, Jedd.   II. Title.
    PN6231.C35H34   2003
    814'.6—dc21

This book is dedicated to

Cherie Hafer,

a mom, grandma, and friend who proves

the truth of the biblical proverb

"The memory of the righteous will be a blessing."

We miss her every day, but every day

we are also grateful for the way her love, support,

and godly example continue to grace our lives.

TODD HAFER, a veteran writer with nineteen books published, is an editorial director for Hallmark, Inc., and lives with his family in Kansas.

JEDD HAFER is a stand-up comic who has performed with some of the top comics in the nation and is also the director of a home for troubled teens. Jedd and his family make their home in Colorado.

Acknowledgments

The authors want to thank, honor, and generally grovel before the following people. . . .

Pastor Del Hafer (our dad) for biblical insight—and for showing us that laughter has a place in church. Although that place isn't the baptistery and doesn't involve a fake shark fin. Sorry about that one, Dad. (Note to readers: Have you ever been spanked with a fake shark fin? It smarts.) Anyway, Pops, you are the best preacher we know, and we admire you and respect your unwavering commitment to your calling.

Keith Stubbs and Robin Krug for comedic inspiration. Thank you for the ideas—and all the laughs. (P.S. When are you going to write *your* books?)

Chip MacGregor and Alive Communications for wise counsel. (That advice to "start using verbs" has really worked for us.)

Steve Taylor, Randy Stonehill, the Swirling Eddies,

Daniel Amos, the Lost Dogs, and all the others who have married music with mirth. You've inspired us and helped us feel less alone.

Carol, Steve, Donna, Julie, Elizabeth, and everyone at Bethany House Publishers. We are grateful to be working with you.

Mark Lowry, Karen Linamen, Sigmund Brouwer, Nichole Nordeman, Bruce & Stan, and Patsy Clairmont for the kind words you've said on our behalf. Encouragement from people like you means so much to us.

Our wives (one for each of us), Jody and Lindsey Hafer, and our kids for believing in us and enduring deadline pressures and odd-hour writing binges. Also, we thank you because when we say, "Stop us if you've heard this one"—and you've heard it—you still let us go ahead and tell the joke.

Finally, a big thanks to the other pastors in our family for all you've taught us about storytelling, comedic timing, Australian Rules Football, and life in general:

The Reverend Chadd Hafer

Chaplain Ron Hafer

The Reverend Jerry Springston

Chaplain Jay Hafer

The Almost-Reverend Bradd Hafer, who ministers to needy children through Compassion International and has a gift for uncovering hope-giving laughter in places where humor is hard to find.

Foreword

I have always been fascinated by the power of humor to bring healing into nearly every area of our lives. After all, humor defuses conflict, enchances communication, combats isolation, and lowers guards. It lifts our spirts, broadens our perspectives, and helps us cope. It even reduces stress, decreases blood pressure, and strengthens immune systems! Best yet, humor has no calories and can't make anyone pregnant, so there are very few downsides to a rip-roaring belly laugh, unless, of course, you consider the embarrassing matter of snorting. Some people laugh until they cry. I laugh until the pigs come home.

Snortage notwithstanding, laughter remains an amazing gift.

As a writer, some of the most poignant, amazing letters I receive are from readers who have discovered the healing properties of humor in the midst of life's most heartbreaking circumstances. I'll never forget the woman who wrote me two days after being diagnosed with breast cancer and told me that, having read a humorous piece I wrote on the therapeutic benefits of TV Land theme songs, she tried to quell her panic by asking her husband to sing the *Gilligan's Island* theme song with her. They went on to spend an hour singing the themes to *Green Acres*, *The Brady Bunch*, and more, until her tears subsided and she was able to fall asleep.

Imagine! In the hands of our creative, loving God, anything is possible: the jawbone of a donkey becomes a weapon of mass destruction, a stable becomes a palace, and a ditty about a man named Brady becomes a pathway to respite from pain.

Laughter really *is* good medicine.

I was in my pastor's office last week and fell madly in love with a framed print on his wall. It's a drawing of Jesus—laughing. Not sporting an enigmatic smile or even a self-righteous grin, but engaged in a full-fledged mouth-open-head-flung-back-eyes-crying sort of belly laugh. Looking at that drawing, I'd wager that before it was over the Lord even let loose a holy snort or two.

Holy snorts. Now, there's a good transition into the work of the Hafer Brothers if there's ever been one. I laughed out loud at their advice to graduating seniors to "never spit in a woman's face . . . unless her mustache is on fire." And you'll just have to mine the pages of this book to discover for yourself what sushi and celebrities have in common, as well as what Todd and Jedd have to say about the new trend in "What Would Jesus Do" eyepatches.

The only bad thing I have to say about this book is based on the fact that I was sitting in a coffeehouse while reading the manuscript. I can't say for sure, but I suspect that a snort ceases to be holy when it causes a woman to spew latte from her nostrils.

Enjoy this book. Whether your life is characterized at the moment by major struggles or mundane stresses, I encourage you to let the pages minister joy and healing to your spirit. Embrace the mirth. Ponder the insights. Laugh out loud.

Just don't drink a latte while doing it.

Karen Linamen

Contents

INTRODUCTION

First, thanks for reading this book. Thanks for buying it—or for receiving it as a gift and not returning it for a bag of tube socks or a carton of cigarettes. We hope we can keep you entertained, or at least awake.

Many of the stories and essays you'll read are from our routines at various comedy clubs, churches, schools, summer camps, corporate team-building functions, and barn-raisings. We're trying to give you stand-up comedy in handy book form. We hope you like *Mischief From the Back Pew*, and we hope that you'll come see us "live" sometime. Our shows have been likened to "getting a hug from Venus de Milo." We hope this book can provide a similar effect.

To enhance your reading pleasure—and because we have almost three "Intro" pages to fill—here are a few things you need to know about *Mischief From the Back Pew*.

1. The stories you are about to read are true. Pretty much. Sure, we embellish here and there, but we do so only after much fasting and soul-searching. And even then, we never spice up a chapter unless we can look each other in the eye and say yes to the question "Will punching up this story make it funnier?"

2. The people in these stories are real, except for Todd's imaginary childhood friend, Cowboy Sam. However, we've changed many of the names to protect the identities of certain individuals— thereby keeping said individuals from pummeling us when they see us at the donut shop. Of course, when we mention someone famous, like Regis Philbin, Miss Universe, or Aunt Jemima, we're talking about the real person. (Yes, we know we're name-dropping here, and we really shouldn't do that. Both Carrot Top and David Hasselhoff have told us we name-drop too much. We think Donny Osmond might have mentioned it, too—at a back-yard barbecue hosted by the Dixie Chicks and Puff Daddy.)

3. We've been in a lot of churches. Our dad is a pastor, and pastors tend to change congregations as often as major league baseball teams change relief pitchers. But for the sake of simplicity, we've condensed our church-related adventures into one: Buffalo Baptist Church. We did this for two reasons. First, it's much shorter than Broomfield/Enid/Cheyenne/Denver/Colorado Springs/Wellington/Buffalo/Green Mountain Falls/Woodland Park/Fort Collins Community Non-Denominational Grace Fellowship Presbyterian Baptist

Church and Home for Troubled Youth.

Second, in our first book we used Broomfield Baptist as our archetypal church, and frankly, the good folks of Broomfield have suffered enough as a result.

4. This book continues the humor saga begun in our first collaboration, *Snickers From the Front Pew*. It's not necessary to read *Snickers* to enjoy *Mischief*. However, we won't discourage you from getting *Snickers* if your inclinations and discretionary income allow.

   In any case, we'd love to hear from you. You can give us your compliments, condemnations, and grooming tips on our Web site, *www.haferbros.com*.

5. If you like *Snickers* and *Mischief*, check out our other collaboration, *How to Overcome Negative Thinking*. (Although frankly, we don't think it's any good.)

1

Sunday Morning at the Improv

Sometimes we like to sit down with our dad and discuss the differences between our careers. He is a pastor. We are comedians/humorists (Jedd at major comedy clubs nationwide, Todd at car wash openings and "celebrity roasts" for assistant managers at local fast-food outlets).

Dad tells us that he sometimes envies the comedy club atmosphere—the energy, and the fact that you usually get lots of free popcorn. He's often fantasized about showing up for open-mike night at a comedy club, billed as "The Reverend of Revelry" or "The Vicar of Snickers." Dad's fantasy got us wondering: What would church be like if it were run like a comedy club? . . .

[Booming voice of head deacon/elder]

"Ladies and gentlemen, welcome to Buffalo Baptist Church! Please keep your pew conversations low and your spirituality high, because it's time to be holy and happy! (And please observe the two-offering minimum.)

"You all know our feature act for this morning. You've seen him at Wednesday Night Bible Study and the weekly

Elders' Meeting. And you've probably seen him mowing the church lawn in sandals, black socks, and powder-blue polyester shorts. Let's give it up for The Minister of Mirth—The Reverend Delllll Haaaaaaa-fer!"

[Rocking intro music by organist]

"Helloooooo, Buffalo! How is everybody doing this morning? Let me tell you, it's good to be here. And hey, let's give it up for Florence "Backbeat" Schneider on the organ! By the way, Florence, Elton John called. He wants his suit back! Hey, just kiddin', Flo! I love ya! Wow, it's great to see my four sons in the congregation today. And to think that some pastors have only ONE pair of loafers!

"Okay, then. Enough about the usual suspects. Any people here from out of town?

"You all know our feature act for this morning. You've seen him mowing the church lawn in sandals, black socks, and powder-blue polyester shorts."

"Great—the family in the front row. Where are you folks from? Texas, eh. Well, let me make you feel at home: Burrrrrrp! [loud belch] Nah, really, I'm just kidding. It's great to have you here. You know, I just got back in town myself. I was at a district meeting for the Northwestern Baptist Convention. Boy, talk about a room full of stiffs! At first I thought I'd made a mistake and gone to the

Arthritis Convention! Let me tell you, these people make Al Gore look like Little Richard!

"It was interesting, though—there was another convention in town the same week. It was a gathering of the Christian Men Without Thumbs. Anyway, they took a vote and everyone agreed—Amy Grant is definitely an '8.'

"Hey, are you people awake? [pounds on mike] Is this thing on? Are you an audience or an oil painting? Ha-ha-ha! Don't make me come down there and 'smite thee'! Anyway, I've been reading my Bible, and how about those Israelites, huh? You know why they wandered for forty years in the wilderness? All the men were too stubborn to stop and ask for directions! Am I right, ladies? Can I get a witness? And speaking of Israelites, that Moses was an interesting character, wasn't he? I can just imagine him arguing with his wife: 'Honey, why must I make all the sacrifices in this family?'

"Hey, look, I see a family just sliding into the back pew. Can I get you folks anything . . . like a watch?!

"I have to tell you, I love this church. It's a lot better than the one I grew up in. What a strict, fear-filled church. They had a sign on their lawn that said 'BEWARE OF GOD.' You want to talk uptight? The stair railings were made of OVER-wrought iron! And those people believed in giving till it hurts. Unfortunately for our pastor, they had a very low pain tolerance. Oh, somebody stop me!

"Hey, you've been great! But I see it's almost time for the elders' meeting. You don't want to cross those guys. They make Clint Eastwood look like Mister Rogers. This is a group of guys who never saw a horse so dead that it didn't deserve one more good beating! Ha! Just kidding. I love you guys. Really. Thanks for helping me make money the old-fashioned way. My salary is the same as it was back in 1968!

"So, anyway, you've been a great congregation—thank you very much! Remember, I'm here every weekend—two shows, 8:30 and 11 A.M. Okay, I'm outta here! Good morning, everybody!"

2

THE PRODIGAL SON (IN THE KEY OF F)

Back in the introduction, we said our dad was the best preacher we know. But then, most preachers' kids say this, especially if their papa-pastor believes in spanking. We weren't boasting idly, however. We truly believe our dad is a gifted communicator with unique ways of connecting with his audiences. One thing we admire is how he can give familiar Bible stories a unique burst of energy and humor.

Our favorite example is Dad's version of the Prodigal Son. This is a piece of Bible storytelling that has been floating around for forty-plus years, and you may have seen various versions of it, but Dad's is our favorite—especially because he keeps tweaking and refining it year after year.

Dad says he first began telling this story before either of us was born, back when he worked for an organization called Youth for Christ. He and some of his fellow YFCers were seeking a way to get kids to settle down and listen to the Word—preferably a way that didn't include tranquilizer darts or handcuffs. Someone had an idea to develop a completely alliterative version of a popular Bible story.

Flummoxed, famished, filled with foreboding, and fairly facing famine, the frazzled fugitive found his faculties and returned to his father's farm.

"The Prodigal Son (in the Key of F)" was the result. We'd like to share it with you now. For the greatest effect, it should be recited rapid-fire, like Dad does.

Feeling footloose, frisky, and fancy-free, a frivolous, feather-brained fellow forced his fond, fawning father to fork over a fair share of the family farthings. Then the flighty flibbertigibbet bade farewell and fled far to foreign fields, where he frittered his fabulous fortune, feasting famously among faithless fair-weather friends until, fleeced by his fun-loving fellows in folly, he found himself a feed-flinger in a festering, filthy farmyard.

Flummoxed, famished, filled with foreboding, and fairly facing famine, the frazzled fugitive found his faculties and returned to his father's farm. "Father, Father!" he forlornly fumbled, "I've flunked, flubbed, failed, and frivolously forfeited family favor. Phooey on me! Let me be as one of your flunkies. For even a fruitless flunkie would fare far, far better than I have fared. Fair enough?"

"Filial fidelity is fine," the father philosophized, "but, folks, the fugitive is found! Let fanfares flare! Let flags unfurl! Fetch the fatling, play that funky music, and let's have some fun!"

Unfortunately, older brother Frank was unforgiving. "Father!" he fumed furiously. "Forsooth from this folly! Frankly, it's unfair. That fool forfeited his fortune!"

"Frank, Frank, Frank, Frank Frank," the father confronted. "Don't fear nor fester. I'm your fan. Your coffers are fairly filled to overflowing, with forty million farthings. But your phantom brother is finally and fortuitously back in the fold. For many fortnights, I've fantasized about this fabulous and festive feast. So focus on fun, not funds—or flake off, Frankie."

So, a fatheaded, foolish fugitive found fulfillment.

Furthermore, the father's fond forgiveness formed the foundation for the former fugitive's future welfare. For a faithful father loves forever.

(We're finally finished!)

3

TV OR NOT TV:
CHRISTIAN COMMERCIALS WE HOPE
WE NEVER SEE

We think it's cool that more and more Christian TV stations are emerging. They can provide a wholesome alternative to the disturbing stuff on the other channels—like those ferocious crocodiles who are always mauling innocent wildebeests on the Discovery Channel. We have only one fear: TV stations need advertisers, and we're afraid that could mean a barrage of ads featuring schlocky Christian products. Products from the same type of people who created the Twelve Disciples Wristwatch ("It's a quarter past Bartholomew—time for Granny to take her meds!") and the Thy Praises Shall Ever Be on My Tongue Toothbrush.

We fear that some night we'll be sitting down to this:

[Booming Matinee-Idol Voice] "We'll be right back to the Heavenly Superstation's presentation of *I Forgive You, My Gangsta Brothers*, starring Jean-Claude Van Darn, the Christian action hero who always turns the other cheek. But first, these messages from our sponsors. . . .

"Hi, I'm Ben-Hur. You know, those full-contact chariot races can be hard on the old bod. That's why Ben-Hur uses Ben-Gay. It soothes my aching muscles and makes me feel warm and tingly all over. It truly is the balm of balms."

"Hello, I'm Noah. I'm here to talk to you about irregularity. As you probably know, irregularity is no fun. It's worse than being cooped up with an ark full of smelly animals. That's why if you're feeling a bit bound up, I urge you to try my new Noah's Laxative—just look for the box with the big rainbow on it. Then take the tablets two by two, and you'll receive up to forty days and forty nights of gentle, effective relief. And that's a promise. Just make sure you're in the right place when the 'flood' hits."

Those full-contact chariot races can be hard on the old bod. That's why Ben-Hur uses Ben-Gay.

"Samson here, folks. As you've probably heard, a guy like me is always on the go. You never know when you might have to sneak out of a city in the middle of the night. That's why I use genuine Samsonian luggage. It's like me—strong, tough, and durable. And because it's easy to clean, you can even haul a dirty old jawbone or a mess o' honey in it. So don't be a Philistine. Ask for Samsonian luggage. Keep an eye out for it at your local store."

"Greetings, folks. I'm Jacob!"

"And I'm Esau. We're here to tell you about the fantastic new Jacob & Esau coat from Land of Canaan Fog."

"That's right, bro. This coat is reversible—furry on the inside and smooth on the outside. Or maybe it's the other way around!"

"That it is, Jake. I like wearing the fur on the outside when I'm in the wild, doing something manly, like hunting. Of course, if you're doing sissy housework, like making soup, I'd go smooth side out."

"That was really uncalled for, Esau. I'm taking my reversible coat and leaving."

"This isn't your coat! It's my coat!"

"You're wrong, gorilla boy!"

"Am not, hairless wonder!"

"I'm telling! Daaaaaad!"

[Booming voice again] ". . . and now we return to *I Forgive You, My Gangsta Brothers*, starring Jean-Claude Van Darn, with Sidney Poitier as Crazy K-Dog Mack-Daddy Washington."

(4)

A Case of the Pre-Concert Chatters[1]

We've always loved Christian music. When we were just kids, Dad bought us Larry Norman and Randy Stonehill records. His only stipulation was that we hide them when the deacons came over. They hated rock music— even Christian rock music. We thought Dad was going to get fired one day when they caught us listening to a Crosby, Stills & Nash album. Luckily, Dad convinced them that the "Crosby" in CS&N was hymn writer extraordinaire Fanny Crosby. "She's trying to get the other two saved," Dad assured them.

Anyway, Dad not only bought us music, he occasionally let us go to Christian concerts—a practice we still enjoy. We always arrive early so that we can get a good seat. Then, after marking our territory, we like to weave through the crowd and hear what people are saying as they await the arrival of the minstrel du jour. Sometimes the conversations are intriguing and revealing. Take these

---

[1] Editor's Note: An adaptation of this selection was chosen for the book *The Best Christian Writing 2000* (San Francisco: HarperSanFrancisco, 2001).

snippets from the fans at a recent Amy Grant concert:

"Hey, I like your WWJD bracelet."

"Why, thank you! I like your WWJD baseball cap."

"So, do you like Amy?"

"Yeah, kinda. Not as much since she's gone secular, though."

"I know what you mean. Who does she think she is?"

★ ★ ★

"Outrageous! So you used to sing with Petra? So did I!"

"Then you might know some of my eight friends here. They are also former chips off the Old Rock!"

★ ★ ★

"What are you reading, Steve?"

"Oh, just an article. Some Christians are coming up with a formula to determine what makes Christian music 'Christian.' "

"Interesting. Maybe when they're done with that, they can come up with a formula for love, beauty, and truth."

"I don't see what the big mystery is. If something doesn't mention Christ or God by name, it's not Christian. Simple as that. Why do you think I tore the books of Esther and Song of Solomon out of my Bible?"

"Steve, dude, you are so discerning and spiritually mature!"

★ ★ ★

"I'm telling ya for the last time—Gary Chapman and Steven Curtis Chapman are not cousins!"

"Yeah, right. Next you're gonna tell me that Phil Keaggy didn't cut off his own finger to impress Jimi Hendrix on *The Merv Griffin Show* in 1972!"

★ ★ ★

"Dude, I love your WWJD tattoo!"

"Yeah, thanks. Nice WWJD eye patch, by the way."

★ ★ ★

"Hey, Angie, is that guy up by the stage a Christian artist? He looks familiar."

"Nah, he's fat, bald, and plain-looking. He couldn't be a Christian artist. You can't put a dude like that on an album cover. I mean, where would you even begin to airbrush him?"

★ ★ ★

"Why the long face, Stacey?"

"Oh, I went to the Christian music store today and ordered the 'True Love Waits' CD. But it's out of stock, so they had to back-order it. It won't be in for six weeks. SIX WEEKS! Can you believe that? That's way, way too long!"

★ ★ ★

"Say, buddy, can you give us some info?"

"Sure."

"Are there any real Australians left in the Newsboys?"

"I think so, mate."

"Thank goodness! Those Aussie accents really minister to us. Incidentally, that's a cool WWJD boomerang you have there."

★ ★ ★

"Homeboy, I don't care what you say! It's simply unspiritual to call Rebecca St. James 'a hottie.' You should be like me and love her like a sister, with absolute reverence. That's why I have all her posters in my room. I revere her, man!"

★ ★ ★

"I sure hope that Amy screams, 'Does anybody here love Jesus?' I love it when Christian artists do that!"

"Yeah, but I hope they don't take a love offering. I spent my last thirty bucks on a T-shirt!"

★ ★ ★

"Yo, Samantha, check it out. Those people over there are dancing! Look at them shimmying and writhing around. It's shameful!"

"Uh, Molly—that's the line for the bathroom."

★ ★ ★

". . . look out! Here comes the WWJD beach ball!"

★ ★ ★

"This announcer bites. Why couldn't they get that 'Let's get ready to rumble' guy?"

"Know what else stinks? You just don't hear very much about backward-masking anymore. It troubles my spirit to think of all the indecipherable-yet-dangerous messages I might be hearing without being aware of them at a meaningful cognitive level."

"eerga I!"

★ ★ ★

"Ouch! Watch where you're throwin' that WWJD Frisbee, you stupid jer—er . . . I mean, my esteemed brother in the Lord!"

★ ★ ★

"Hold me close, Ted. There are *secular* people here. I've seen eight shirts with naughty words on them!"

"It's okay, honey. You know, I'm kinda ticked at Amy. If she hadn't gotten so popular, we wouldn't have to deal with these pagan reprobates."

★ ★ ★

"Dude, what are those protesters doing out by the concert entrance?"

That Christian heavy-metal concert rocked! I loved it when that guy smashed his guitar as unto the Lord!

"You don't know? Amy has done some ads for Target. And Target sells Pringles potato chips. And one of the companies that provides the plastic used to make the resealable Pringles canister tops has a guy named Fred on its executive board. And that Fred guy is known to drink Zima and watch PG-13 movies!"

"No kidding? Man, Amy should be more careful whom she associates with!"

"I hope this concert is loud. My ears are still ringing from the Christian heavy-metal concert last month."

"Yeah, that concert rocked! I loved it when that guy smashed his guitar as unto the Lord!"

★ ★ ★

"Jill, all this WWJD stuff has got me thinking. What *would* Jesus do if He were here tonight?"

"Well, Amanda, there are a lot of Christians here— and a lot of non-Christians, too. And we're here in search of something that will connect with all of us, without alienating any of us. So my guess is that He would do something very much like what Amy is about to do."

"But what about . . ."

"Shhhh. Here she comes. It's time to stop criticizing and just listen. . . ."

5

CHRISTIANESE AS A SECOND LANGUAGE

Do you have any "praises to share"? Are you feeling "convicted" about anything? Do you need "traveling mercies" for a trip you are taking soon? When was the last time you "sat under the teaching" of a godly individual? In short, are you "living victoriously"?

If you struggled to answer any of these questions, perhaps your Christianese isn't as sharp as it should be. At BBC, many in our congregation pride themselves on their eloquent Christianese. After all, how can one of "God's chosen lambs" expect to "fellowship" with other believers if one isn't fluent in the language?

If you're "troubled in your spirit" about this issue, we can help.

Because we want to "encourage you in your daily pilgrimage," we've developed an impressive educational chart to assist you in your pursuit of expert Christianese. We must say that it is in no way to be viewed as "exhaustive." (Why would you want to read something that makes you tired, anyway?) But we believe this little cheat sheet will do until you feel comfortable in the deep waters of Lake Christianese.

---

*H*ow can one of "God's chosen lambs" expect to "fellowship" with other believers if one isn't fluent in the language?

So the next time you're asked, "How is your walk?" or "In what way are you gifted in the Spirit?" just refer to the chart and choose the combinations of Christianese jargon that best suit your needs. Good luck—oops, we mean Godspeed, our beloved brothers and sisters!

The Hafer Brothers' Handy Christianese Chart

Part 1	Part 2	Part 3
I'm as blessed	as Amy Grant	eating a jelly donut!
I'm as sanctified	as a bald choir director	sitting on an old hymnal!
I'm as under conviction	as a youth pastor	with an overly critical spirit!
I'm as discerning	as a Naugahyde pew cushion	in a velvet choir robe!
I'm as spiritual	as a pastoral search committee	in a church van leaking oil!
I'm as encouraged	as a minor prophet	in a cold baptistery!

I'm as reverent	as a televangelist	ministering among cannibals!
I'm as compassionate	as a nursery volunteer	at an inerrancy debate!
I'm as evangelistic	as a covered side dish	watching *The 700 Club*!
I'm as uplifted	as a bell choir	in a nursery full of dirty diapers!
I'm as worshipful	as a church organist	at a Christian singles night!
I'm as edified	as a visiting missionary	at a Gaithers reunion concert!

Are you getting the hang of this Christianese thing? Do you see how easy it can be to "share" just like all the super-spiritual people you see on Christian TV? If this list can help you babble like a true believer, we'll be as "humbled as an interim Sunday school superintendent playing an offertory on a kazoo"!

6

Mamas, Don't Let Your Babies Grow Up to Be Cowboy Fans

(or, The Hafer Brothers' Ongoing Spiritual Struggle with "The Chaplain of America's Team")

The Hafer Boys were raised on football. We could recite the teams in the AFC and NFC before we could recite the alphabet. And while most kids' first sentences were something like "The red ball is on the doggie," ours were along the lines of "Give me a break, ref, there was a lineman illegally downfield on that halfback pass!"

Thus, some of our earliest memories are of gathering around the TV set on Sunday afternoons and watching the Denver Broncos get creamed. (But remember, that was in the mid-1970s, before they became the most dominant team in the history of competitive athletics. Go, Broncos! Denver Broncos ruuuuule!)

Unfortunately, some of those memories are tainted, just like the burgers at . . . uh, well, you know! Sometimes, you see, Charles "Chuck" Charles would invade our home right before the opening kick-off. And Charles was a Dallas Cowboy fan. He was known throughout Buffalo—and even in parts of Casper and Cheyenne—as "The Chaplain of the Cowboys."

Charles[2] would lower his ample hindquarters into the special Hafer Guest Metal Folding Chair and immediately begin dissing the men in orange and blue.

"A Cowboy receiver would have caught that one," he'd say after a dropped Denver pass. Or, "Roger Staubach could have avoided that sack, due to his superior mobility. Your quarterback runs like a duck."

Even if the Broncos managed to win, Chuck would offer only the faintest whisper of praise: "Not a bad game for a bunch of mediocre players. Now, the Cowboys would have destroyed the opposition. The game would have been over in the first quarter. You see, my naïve Bronco backers, the Dallas Cowboys are America's Team. In fact, they are God's Team."

To this day, our hearts ache when the Broncos lose. But the pain is even greater when the Cowboys win.

Chuck's constant taunting and patronizing made us want to hate him. But Dad said we couldn't hate anyone in the church—especially a guy who tithed as faithfully as Chuck. (Probably with the money he won betting on his beloved team.) So we hated the Cowboys instead.

We admit it: To this day, our hearts ache when the Broncos lose. But the pain is even greater when the Cowboys win. Especially if Chuck happens to be watching the game with us. He still comes over occasionally to view the gridiron action with us—and test the strength and durability of our trusty folding guest chair.

He was almost tolerable for a while—during the years when the Cowboys stunk like a hamper full of the New Orleans Saints' sweat socks. He'd just shake his head and say, "God's Team is being tested. This is a time of trials and tribulations for us, but as Ed 'Too Tall' Jones is my witness, we shall overcome."

Sadly for us, it appears the Cowboys are experiencing a resurgence. They have a new coach, and their talent pool is slowly deepening. We fear that someday soon, the 'Boys will be as good as they were when we were mere children, booing them mercilessly.

Ah, we remember those days with angst. Dallas had guys like Troy Aikman and Moose Johnston. Then they added Deion Sanders to their corral. They signed him to a zillion-dollar contract, making them even deadlier on both sides of the ball. It was not fair. Why did Dallas have to get "Prime Time"? (For the gridiron-impaired, that's Deion's nickname. It's catchy because it rhymes and everything.)

Every Sunday during the Deion era, Charles[2] would tell us, "This season is just a formality. The NFL should just give the Cowboys their Super Bowl rings right now. God bless America's Team. God bless God's Team. Amen."

We confess that we didn't demonstrate a Christian attitude in those days. We referred to Prime Time as "Prime Rib," "Prime Number," and even "Primer Coat." And we said things like, "Sure, Prime the Pump is a great cover man. But he can't tackle anybody. Alice from *The*

Brady Bunch hits harder than he does." For comments like these, we repent before Mr. Sanders and earnestly request that he not beat us up when he sees us at the next Christian Booksellers Convention.

Neon Deion is long gone now, but to Chuck, the Cowboys are still ready for prime time. He continues to herd many of the BBC congregation into the Dallas corral. Now even nominal football fans are hugging Chuck in the foyer and hollering things like "Hurray for the Cowboys!" or "Hey, I've been a Dallas fan all along!" or "Go, Lone Star State!"

We cringe at such proclamations. Because today's Cowboys are not the team they were back when they had our begrudging admiration. To us, the new-millennium Cowboys represent much of what is wrong with the world.

For example, during a game this past season, an opposing wide receiver returned the opening kickoff to his team's 35-yard line—a respectable return—before two Cowboys nudged him out of bounds. On this play, the Cowboys' opponents won. The Dallas goal was to stop them inside the 20. But what did the Cowboys do? They jumped up and down and high-fived each other as if they had perfected the process of cold fusion or secured a double date with Cameron Diaz and Jennifer Love Hewitt.

This is the kind of team Dallas has become. In another game, a Cowboy defensive back got burned for a first down but then caught up with the receiver, tackled him after a twenty-five-yard gain, and then did a little dance, as if to say, "Aren't I something? I tackled a guy! I hit him hard!" Boogie all you want, drugstore Cowboy; the first-down chains still move.

Chuck roars with delight at this cocky, demonstrative behavior. But we don't understand it. The Cowboys are merely doing their jobs. We don't see McDonald's employees dancing around and shouting, "The McNuggets are done! Yippee! Group hug!"

Come on, Cowboys, where's the humility? Legendary Dallas quarterback Roger Staubach would roll over in his grave, except he's not dead.

Despite all the arrogance, the Cowboy bandwagon keeps taking on more people, and Chuck is the guy yelling, "All aboard!" Maybe the whole thing should be called The Cowboy Chuck-Wagon.

A few Sundays ago, Chuckster stood in Fellowship Hall, pontificating about his Lone Star warriors to a large group of Buffalo Baptist Church attendees, when Jedd's tolerance snapped like a dry twig.

"Okay, Chuck, you win," Jedd said sarcastically. "Let's all be Cowboy fans. After all, they are God's Team. And while we're at it, let's all root for the Atlanta Braves and the Los Angeles Lakers, too! Let's all chant, 'I was born and raised in a briar patch'! Let's all listen to Celine Dion, drink Sprite, and watch *Survivor* and *American Idol*! Let's all sing 'The stars at night / are big and bright / deep in the heart of Texas' as our opening hymn every Sunday. Let's avoid thinking for ourselves! Let's all be brain-dead!"

Chuck smiled sadly and shook his Stetson-topped head. "The words of a jealous, bitter Bronco fan," he observed. "The words of someone who knows that the

Cowboys will win the next Super Bowl. Am I right, 'pard-ners'?"

Chuckster's disciples hollered in unison: "Right you are! Yippie-ky-aye! Get along, little dogies!"

Wrong. The Cowboys will not win the next Super Bowl—even if Prime Time comes out of retirement and rejoins the team. Here's something we want Charles[2] and all the rest of you Cowboy fans to hear. We predict that the Dallas gridders will not win the next Super Bowl. We're not saying they won't win eleven games and get to the playoffs, because they probably will. But something will stop them. We don't know what it will be. Perhaps it will be the Hafer Brothers imposing their collective will on the Cowbuckaroos.

So now we are accountable to you, Dallas players and fans. If the guys from the Lone Star State win it all next year, we'll apologize. We'll Turtle-Wax Chuck's pickup truck. We'll issue a public apology. We'll slap Cowboy bumper stickers on our cars for the entire shelf life of a Ding Dong (approximately 88.2 years).

However, if the Cowboys don't get to the Big Dance, we will wave Bronco-orange towels over our heads, douse ourselves in Gatorade, and slurp Orange Crush from our John Elway commemorative mugs as we celebrate on Chuck's front lawn—just as if we had accomplished some-thing amazing. Then, perhaps, the Chaplain of the Cowboys will regain his grasp on reality and say a final benediction on this whole America's Team/God's Team nonsense.

BULLETIN BLOOPERZ

Ah, the church bulletin (or "program," for you sports fans). Bulletins are integral to any church service. They provide an outline for the sermon. They alert parishioners to upcoming events. And they can serve as the playing field for a mid-church game of tic-tac-toe or hangman during a lull in the sermon. (For more on this last topic, see the chapter titled "Things To Do During a Dull Sermon.")

But for us, the church bulletin's best feature is to provide unexpected laughs when those who prepare the bulletins don't think carefully about—or proofread—their work before sending it off to the printer—or to the hand-operated mimeograph machine, in BBC's case.

During his years as a pastor, our dad has collected his favorite Bulletin Bloopers—and our church has done its part to keep the list growing. If you have some gems that you don't read here, please send them to us at *www.haferbros.com*. We'll put the best ones in our next book.

Pastor Hafer's Unofficial List
of Favorite Bulletin Bloopers

- Our church will host a potluck dinner tonight, featuring live music. This promises to be a memorable evening for both the young and the young in heat.
- Bertha Belch, a missionary from Africa, will be speaking tonight at Calvary Memorial Church in Racine. Come tonight and hear Bertha Belch all the way from Africa.
- Don't forget next month's Prayer & Fasting conference. Registration is only $50, and the price includes all meals and snacks.
- Our youth basketball team is back in action Friday at 8 P.M. in the recreation hall. Come out and watch us stomp The Sacred Heart of Mary.
- Ladies, don't forget the rummage sale. It's a chance to get rid of those things not worth keeping around the house. Don't forget to bring your husbands.
- Next Sunday is the family hayride and bonfire at the Fowlers'. Bring your own hot dogs and guns. Friends are welcome! Everyone come for a fun time.
- The peacemaking meeting scheduled for today has been canceled due to a conflict.
- The sermon this morning: "Jesus Walks on the Water." The sermon for tonight: "Searching for Jesus."
- Remember the big all-church swap meet next Saturday in City Park. Husbands, bring your wives and get a great bargain!
- Next Thursday there will be tryouts for the choir. They need all the help they can get.

- Barbara remains in the hospital and needs blood donors for more transfusions. She is also having trouble sleeping and requests tapes of Pastor Jack's sermons.
- The rector will preach his farewell message tonight, after which the choir will sing "Break Forth Into Joy."
- Just a reminder, the lavatory on the upper level is broken; please go in the basement.
- Remember in prayer the sick of our church and community. Smile at someone who is hard to love. Say "hell" to someone who doesn't care much about you.
- Don't let worry kill you—let the church help.
- On Thursday there will be a meeting of the Little Mothers Club. All wishing to become Little Mothers, please Deacon Sanders in the Fellowship Hall after the morning service.
- This being Easter Sunday, we will ask Mrs. Lewis to come forward and lay an egg on the altar.
- Irving Benson and Jessie Carter were married on October 24 in the church. So ends a friendship that began in their school days.
- A bean supper will be held on Tuesday evening in the church hall. Music will follow.
- At the evening service tonight, the sermon topic will be "What is Hell?" Come early and listen to our choir practice.
- Eight new choir robes are currently needed due to the addition of several new members and the deterioration of some older ones.
- The senior choir invites any member of the congregation who enjoys sinning to join us right away!
- Our boy scouts are saving aluminum cans, bottles, and

other items to be recycled. Proceeds will be used to cripple children.

---

*F*or those of you who have children and don't know it, we have a nursery downstairs.

- The Lutheran men's group will meet tomorrow at 6 P.M. Steak, mashed potatoes, green beans, bread, and dessert will be served for a nominal feel.
- For those of you who have children and don't know it, we have a nursery downstairs.
- Please place your donation in the envelope along with the deceased person(s) you want remembered.
- Attend our prayer breakfast next Saturday, and you will hear an excellent speaker and heave a hearty meal.
- Don't forget, on New Year's Eve the church will host an evening of fine dining, superb entertainment, and gracious hostility.
- Potluck supper Sunday at 5:00 P.M. Prayer and medication to follow.
- The ladies of the church have cast off clothing of every kind. They may be seen in the basement on Friday afternoon.
- This evening at 7 P.M. there will be a hymn sing in the park across from the church. Bring a blanket and come prepared to sin.
- The Ladies Bible Study will be held Thursday morning

at 10. All ladies are invited to lunch in the Fellowship Hall after the B.S. is done.

- The pastor would appreciate it if the ladies of the congregation would lend him their electric girdles for the pancake breakfast next Sunday morning.
- Our Low-Self-Esteem Support Group will meet Thursday at 7 P.M. (Please use the back door.)
- Next Sunday afternoon, Farmer Jones will host our youth, giving them a behind-the-scenes tour of his diary.
- The eighth graders will be presenting Shakespeare's *Hamlet* in the church basement Friday at 7 P.M. The entire congregation is invited to attend this tragedy.
- Weight Watchers will meet at 7 P.M. at the First Presbyterian Church. Please enter through the large double doors at the side of the building.
- Please remember to pray for Mrs. Johnson, who will be entering the hospital this week for testes.
- Hungry? Then come pot-licking with us in the Fellowship Hall after the service next Sunday!
- Reminder: Housing is needed for the visiting missions drama team next week. If you can put up with these folks for a day or two, please notify the pastor.
- The associate minister unveiled the church's new tithing campaign slogan last Sunday: "I Upped My Pledge—Up Yours!"

8

A Day in the Life . . .

"Boy, I envy you, Pastor Hafer," a visitor from Arkansas told our dad a few Sundays ago. "I wish I could work only one day a week!"

Our dad just flashed his famous grimace-smile and willed himself to keep from crushing the guy's hand like an empty pop can. He hears comments like this all the time, and he's become used to it. We urge him to be more vocal about all his job entails—the late-night counseling sessions, the ministerial association conventions, the weddings, the funerals, the exhaustive search for Sunday school volunteers, the unclogging of the church's kitchen drain, the re-shingling of the sanctuary roof, and so on.

But he just shrugs us off. "God knows all that I'm doing, and that's what matters to me," he says.

We wish we were that spiritually mature. But we're not. We think it's time that someone pulled back the proverbial curtains and revealed the hidden work/life of the people in the pulpit. (A heavy-duty, oak-reinforced pulpit in our dad's case. Sometimes he likes to hammer home his

points with a cantaloupe-sized fist.)

So last Saturday we asked our dad to keep a journal of his workday, noting how he spent the hours and highlighting significant events. Below is the result. We hope it will help all of us non-preacher-folk to have a bit more empathy and compassion for our men and women of the cloth.

Reverend Del Hafer: Spiritual Journal for Saturday, November 1

6:30 A.M.   Some days I wake up thinking, "Good morning, Lord!" On others it's more like, "Good Lord, it's morning!" Today is one of the latter. I'm fatigued. It's been a long week. But there are people who need me. Help me to be strong for them.
P.S. Would it be spiritually immature to pray that there are some of those miniature powdered-sugar donuts left in the church pantry? Thank you.

7:20 A.M.   Arrive at church to ensure that the baptistery is filled with [warm!] water for tomorrow's baptismal service.

7:21 A.M.   Stick arm in baptistery. Pull it back in shock at the arctic water temperature. Call the Scuba Safari Shoppe to see if they rent wetsuits. Wonder if wearing a wetsuit under my baptismal robe will make me look too "chunky."

7:24 A.M.   Stop to notice handmade poster on the rest-
              room door. It's a drawing of Moses with the
              caption, in large, crayon-scrawled letters,
              LET MY PEOPLE GO! Decide to leave the
              poster up. A pastor should always encour-
              age junior-high kids to express their creativ-
              ity.

7:25 A.M.   On the way to my office, I pass the nursery
              and note a similar poster. This one is simply
              text from 1 Corinthians 15:51: "We will not
              all sleep, but we will all be changed . . ."
              This makes me smile. At first I think one of
              my kids created this sign, but then I note
              that this couldn't be the case: The sign is
              legible, and all of the words are spelled cor-
              rectly.

7:45 A.M.   Inspired by the posters, I decide to play a
              joke on "Backbeat Florence," the organist,
              by turning the volume on her electric organ
              to "11"—with a driving rock 'n' roll beat.
              Can't wait till she fires up this baby at the
              beginning of tomorrow's service.

8:01 A.M.   Check phone messages. Only one new one.
              It's from Rabbi Brill, who says, "Hey there,
              Rev-Man, this is your old buddy, the rabbi. I
              was supposed to give an invocation before
              the chili-eating contest next Wednesday.
              Could you pinch-hit for me? And if you
              can, what's your yarmulke size?"

8:20 A.M.   Lord, I hope I didn't just make a big mistake. A panhandler knocked at the church door a few minutes ago. I gave him all the money I had on me—nine dollars and thirteen cents. I pray that he will use the funds for food—not cigarettes, drugs, alcohol, or lottery tickets. But if he does buy lottery tickets and wins millions of dollars, may he donate at least some of his winnings to the church. As you know, we need a new furnace, and the roof leaks when it rains.

9:42 A.M.   Call Mrs. Gackout to remind her that she is to provide the "ministry in music" tomorrow. She says she has her kazoo rendition of "A Mighty Fortress Is Our God" down cold.

9:52 A.M.   Well, Lord, I just had an interesting experience. I went upstairs when I heard a sound coming from the sanctuary. I found Timmy Graham hiding inside the pulpit. He looked scared. He told me that he was hiding from "Shirley Goodness and Mercy," two women his mother said would follow him all the days of his life. I explained that his mom was just quoting the song "Surely Goodness and Mercy." I hope he feels better now. A kid shouldn't have to fear Goodness and Mercy. There are already more than enough scary things in this world.

10:01 A.M.   Timmy just came back, Lord. He was thinking about the "Surely Goodness" hymn, and it sparked a question in his young mind. He said that he now understood what "Surely Goodness" was all about, but he didn't understand the hymn "Gladly the Cross-Eyed Bear." He asked me why we would sing about an optically challenged bear in church. I told him that the hymn was actually "Gladly the Cross I'd Bear." And now he's REALLY confused. Lord, help me to explain to Timmy the concept of bearing one's cross. It's hard for him to understand. And I must confess, I struggle with that one myself sometimes.

1:28 P.M.   Return from taking the vacation Bible school kids to Chuck E. Cheese for lunch and games. I don't remember much about the past couple of hours—except that there were spilled drinks, cold pizza, and lots of noise. And, at one point, I was hugged by a guy in a giant rat suit. For this I thank you, Lord. I needed a hug today. Even if it was from a seven-foot rodent.

2:02 P.M.   Mrs. Tompkins calls to say thanks for taking the kids to Chuck E. Cheese. She also tells me, proudly, that her eight-year-old daughter, Lily, saved two of her Chuck E. Cheese

tokens, which she plans to tithe tomorrow. "Render unto Chuck E.?" she says. "Not in the Tompkins household!" I know that Phil the Treasurer will freak when he sees those tokens in the offering basket tomorrow; help me remember to remind him that they are tokens of a little girl's love.

---

*H*eavenly Father, is it religiously correct to exercise here by bench-pressing my set of Exhaustive Bible Commentaries?

2:30 P.M.   The afternoon is slipping away, and I still have much to do today. I'm not going to be able to make it to the gym. Heavenly Father, is it religiously correct to exercise here by bench-pressing my set of Exhaustive Bible Commentaries? Just wondering . . .

3:59 P.M.   Just got an interesting call from one of my favorite parishioners, Mrs. Opal. She was confused about the church's upcoming cantata. I reassured her that a cantata is a musical presentation, not a potluck dinner with a Mexican-food theme, so she didn't need to make any of her Famous Tamales. I got quite a chuckle out of the whole thing. Thanks for sending some merriment my way, Lord. *Olé!*

5:01 P.M. Well, Lord, my day here at the office should be ending, but my work isn't done. I can't believe it's already past five o'clock. I look forward to heaven, where there won't be so much time pressure. Up there with you, it will always be 4-ever o'clock!

6:38 P.M. Heavenly Father, I am hungry and tired. I want to go home, but as I've been working on tomorrow's sermon, I've become increasingly dissatisfied with it. I've titled it "How to Be Bold and Confident in Christ," but I'm not sure it's any good. I don't know if the congregation will like it. Oh well, I read somewhere that if we will just attempt to walk with you, you will be pleased even with our stumbles. So, Lord, please help me tomorrow. Help me to (at the very least) stumble along in a way that pleases you. Thank you for listening, now and always. Amen.

9

The Name of the Game Is Fame

Every now and then, people from our church (mostly kids, because the adults don't talk to us much) ask us, "What's it like to be famous authors?"

We smile and say something like, "It's fun, but not as much fun as being a kid."

"But my mom says you *are* kids," one of the precious children will offer. "She says it all the time: 'Those Hafer yay-hoos are a couple of overgrown kids.' "

At this point we laugh good-naturedly, then slink away to see if any of the good cookies are left in Fellowship Hall. We slink not at being referred to as big, goofy juveniles; that is pretty much true. It's the fame thing that causes our slinkage. You see, even though we've written a few books and been interviewed on almost every thousand-watt radio station in the country, we are not famous. We are obscure—as obscure as Donna Mulligan.

"Who is Donna Mulligan?" you ask. Well, you've never heard of her, because she is obscure, just like us. See, that's our whole point.

"That's all hunky and dory," you counter. "That Donna Mulligan analogy was intriguing. But it's built on a faulty premise. Donna Mulligan probably hasn't done all of those radio interviews like you have."

And here is where we win the argument. "How can we be obscure?" we ask rhetorically. Well, go look at your toaster. Go ahead; it's all right. We'll wait for you. . . .

Okay, we're still waiting. . . .

Fine, then. It's obvious to us that you are not going to go look at your toaster, and we don't want to get into a big dramatic standoff with you. But if you did go look at your toaster, you'd probably find that it pulls more watts than most of the radio stations that feature us. We are usually interviewed on stations that can be heard clearly only east of the feed store and only on a calm, windless night.

"But," you might ask, "what about the TV interviews, the signings at bookstores?"

True, we have been on TV a fair bit. But we're usually featured on small-market morning shows, with titles like *Good Morning, Butte, Montana*, with Mike, Maddie, and Wally the Wonder Woodchuck. These shows typically air so early in the morning that even the roosters aren't up yet. (Not that roosters would be interested in watching us anyway.)

As for the bookstore signings, we have found that we just don't have the star power to attract many visitors. The few people who do trickle in to our in-store appearances often mistake us for salespeople. Instead of "You are the world's most brilliant humorists; would you please sign a copy of your book—and our infant daughter's forehead?" we hear "Can you show us to the Precious Moments figurines?" or "Excuse me, boys, where is your rest room?"

After an hour or two, the bookstore managers start shooting us hostile glares. We note the resentment in their eyes and know just what they're thinking: "You two light-weight funny-boys aren't fit to trim the stray hairs on Jerry Jenkins' beard. Why, you couldn't draw flies if I rolled you in horse manure!"

Those managers are right. The only Hafer Brothers in-store event that drew more people than flies was for our book *Snickers From the Front Pew*—and that was because our publisher provided hundreds of Snickers candy bars to all visitors. (With that lone success in mind, we tried to title the book you are holding *Butterfingers & Twenty-Dollar Bills From the Back Pew*, but that didn't make it past the Bethany House editors.)

So, we trust we've made our point. We're not famous. We are not household names even in our own households, where our wives refer to us as "Hey, Idiot!"

Most of the time we accept our roles as relatively obscure authors. We are grateful for our small but loyal following. We thank God for the privilege of writing books. We love our readers. We treasure every kind email and letter we receive, even those that are written on the backs of kids' menus from Denny's—in purple crayon.

But once in a while we'll be watching E! (or even a network with two or three letters) and see the big-name authors hobbing and nobbing with movie stars at galas—or being mobbed by adoring fans at a signing at Mega Book Super-Duper Warehouse.

At times like these, fame's aroma entices us, like . . . like . . . something that smells really, really enticing. And we are forced to admit: We wanna be famous! There—we said it, and we're not ashamed.

> *We want our names to be called at the Book o' the Year Awards so that we can look surprised—then do the special cool handshake we rehearsed for weeks.*

In fact, now that it's out there on the table, we are beginning to crave fame. Yeah, fame is where it's at. Fame is what we truly want, no doubt about it. Fame: We like it, we love it, we want more of it! The Hafer Brothers and fame? We would get along famously. Specifically . . .

We want to win major honors and accolades. We want our names to be called at the Book o' the Year Awards so that we can look surprised—then do the special cool handshake we rehearsed for weeks. We want to sprint to the podium and grab a pair of big, shiny, gold-plated awards shaped like Max Lucado's pancreas. We want to give a brief but moving acceptance speech, concluding with ". . . and most of all, we give props to the Big Dude Upstairs!" (This way, people will think we're cool *and* spiritual.)

Then we'll take our statuettes home and place them proudly on our mantels, displacing those amateurish pieces of pottery our kids made at vacation Bible school.

Next, we'll part ways with Chip, our loyal, hard-working,

and service-oriented agent, in favor of a loud and pushy New York agent with a Rolodex the size of a monster-truck tire. Someone who will call us "Hoss" and "Chief" and telephone us all hours of the day and night. That way, we can interrupt our Wednesday-night Bunko games and family devotions and tell everyone loudly, "Sorry. This other stuff will have to wait. We gotta take this call; it's our AGENT—calling from the Big Apple!"

And no more of those basic disposable-camera photos on our book jackets. We want to be in full living color, and we want to be airbrushed. We want our smiling countenances to sport no zits, no lines around our eyes, no blemishes—in fact, no pores.

Furthermore, we want clothes and hair stylists. We want to wear labels that proclaim Gucci, Armani, and Lauren, not "Slightly Irregular—50% Off!" Sure, we'll still be a couple of lanky doofuses (or is it doofi?), but we'll be the best-dressed, best-looking lanky doofuses in the land!

We want to be invited to all the cool mega-parties, where we'll pretend to like sushi and celebrities (even though in reality, we find both to be cold, slimy, and lacking in taste).

We want to make wildly unreasonable demands when we appear in concert. Backstage we want Twinkies with the cream filling removed, then replaced by goose-liver pâté; hickory-smoked reindeer jerky; frozen mink on a stick; fresh yak milk; and buckets and buckets o' purple Skittles. And after every performance, we'll require a mentholated foot rub from Point of Grace.

And no more post-concert meals at Denny's. We won't deign to dine at regular restaurants. After all, those places are for regular people. So everywhere we go, we'll be accompanied by Fuji, the world's best stir-fry guy, and the world-renowned Ernesto, French Toast Master Chef.

After eating sumptuous meals from the hands of Fuji and Ernesto, we'll retire to our luxury hotel suites, where we'll watch ESPN with members of the Minnesota Vikings, who follow us everywhere, declaring, "If there were a Super Bowl for laughs, you homeboys would win it for sure!"

Later, after we've excused the Vikings for the night, we'll become surly and trash our hotel rooms. (However, since we will still be good Christians, "trashing" for us will mean refusing to fill out the comment cards.)

But just because we won't destroy hotel property doesn't mean we won't be controversial. Because we will. (Be controversial, we mean.) In interviews, we'll say inflammatory things like "You know, that I Can't Believe It's Not Butter is *better* than the real thing!" and "Who needs rhetorical questions?!"

Thus, we'll be attacked by everyone from Jerry Falwell to Jerry Jenkins to Jerry Seinfeld to Jerry Springer. But we'll be gracious to all our critics so that everyone will see that we are spiritual Super-Men. We'll even be gracious to Joan Rivers and her daughter, Melissa, when they make fun of our clothes on the E! network. We'll be tempted to say, "Joan, baby, you're making fun of the way *we* look? Have you gazed into a mirror lately? And by the way, Melissa is totally carrying you!" But we'll fight the temptation. We'll just smile bravely and keep truckin' on down the highway of success and maturity—in a chartreuse stretch limousine powered by our own sense of self-importance.

Of course, at every stop along the way, we'll be mobbed by adoring fans. We will smile at them, shake their hands, and say meaningful things like "Keep rockin' for Jesus, yo!" before ducking into our limo and sanitizing our hands.

Ultimately, we want to have the privilege of getting tired and bored of our adoring fans and all the love they heap upon us. We will respond by moving into an exclusive gated community that requires a retinal scan and saliva sample to gain access. From our protective fortress, we will speak to fans via the media. *Christian People Magazine* will put our well-tanned but slightly worried faces on the cover, above the title "The Hafer Brothers Plea to Fans: 'Leave Us Alone, But Keep Buying Our Books, 'Cuz We Love Ya!' "

When even this doesn't serve to place us on a pedestal so high that our followers can't touch the bottoms of our panda-skin boots, we will undergo extensive plastic surgery, so that we look like hybrids of Joan Collins and Michael Jackson. And then we'll get phone numbers so unlisted that even we don't know what they are.

But still our journey o' fame won't be complete. Not even close. We want to get into a bitter brotherly feud rooted in "creative differences." The conflict will become so heated that we'll eventually disown each other. Our fans will become divided, many siding with Jedd when he reveals on a "very special episode" of *Jerry Springer*, "I'm the true creative genius in this duo. And besides, when I was only two, Todd stole my blankie!"

Our notoriety will hits its peak when we are featured on the hot new TV show *Behind the Comedy*. At the show's dramatic conclusion, Todd will return a Taiwan-made replica of Jedd's long-lost blankie to him, and Jedd will use it to dab the tears from his grateful, ocean-blue eyes.

Then, with our popularity spiking to an all-time high, we will demonstrate our true artistic spirit by abandoning our now-household names in favor of symbols. Jedd will be @#$&*, while Todd will be simply %. And just when the press and the public get used to these monikers, we shall take on the new identity of The Brothers Formerly Known as Hafer, Then Known for a Little While as @#$&* and %.

At this point we will become bored with the prospect of entertaining and confusing our fans. Thus, we will spend most of our time eating deep-fried Twinkies and purchasing imported luncheon meats on eBay. We will be too bloated and lethargic to create new material, so we will force our publishers to release a series of "best-of" books and comedy recordings—at prices as inflated as our ever-growing egos.

As a result, even our most loyal fans will begin to desert us. But that's okay. We want that to happen, too. Because we want the chance to show that we don't need the fans anyway. "They never understood our comedy; they didn't deserve us," we'll tell Maury and Ricki and Oprah. "We're above being hurt by the little people."

We won't even become upset when *Christian People Magazine* does another cover story on us, this time titled "The Humorists Formerly Known as Relevant." And we'll forgive Yanni when he fails to invite us to his annual summer corn roast and volleyball extravaganza.

We'll forgive our former and soon-to-be-former fans, too, when they fail to recognize us in the supermarket or bowling alley. After all, we know we must pity them. They simply lack the capacity to appreciate our true genius.

It will still give us a thrill, though, when—despite the plastic surgery and added pounds—a hint of recognition sparkles in a former fan's eyes as we meet at dinnertime at the Chuckwagon Diner and she asks, "Hey, don't I know you guys? Aren't you celebrities or something?"

To which we'll smile and say, "No, we aren't celebrities or even something. But we used to be. Ah yes, indeed. We used to be FAMOUS!"

"Oh," she'll say, "that's nice. Could you take these dirty plates away and bring me a dessert menu?"

"Certainly," Jedd will respond. "I'll be right back, Ms. uh, uh . . ."

"Mulligan's the name. Donna Mulligan. Remember it, because someday I'm gonna be famous! More famous than you ever were!"

Role Models or Parole Models?

Our dad has always used sports illustrations in his sermons, and with good reason. In myriad ways, sports are a microcosm of life. In both there are winners and losers. Both demonstrate the need for teamwork and cooperation. Both reward those who persevere. And in both, men wear silly pants that are either ridiculously too big and baggy or painfully too small and fit like sausage casings.

Another reason that Dad uses sports analogies and illustrations is that it keeps the men in the congregation awake and focused. If he sees a few eyelids falling to half-mast, the Reverend Del Hafer will lean into the microphone and say, "In the words of Hammerin' Hank Aaron . . ." or "You know, my friends, the apostle Paul really reminds me of Rocky Marciano."

Yes, sports are often a pastor's best friend. When a sermon is in the bottom of the ninth and boredom threatens to defeat the congregation, there's nothing like being able to call upon the trusty sports analogy. Like a reliable relief pitcher, the sports analogy is always ready to sprint from the bullpen, step into the pulpit, and save the day. (Come to think of it, those sports analogies can be a writer's best friend, too.)

Unfortunately for our dad and the country's other sports-mad pastors, the world of athletics may no longer be sermon fodder—or even men's-retreat fodder. You see, and we say this with tears welling in our *SportsCenter*-glazed eyes, the world of sports and the world of reality are walking divergent paths. The "human drama of athletic competition" is becoming "the bizarre soap opera of chemically enhanced louts showing preposterous levels of greed, ego, and poor sportsmanship."

Consider the following four trends, and see if you don't agree with us.

1. Professional athletes have lost the distinction between being a showman and a show-off. Recently we were watching a pre-season NFL game featuring the Oakland Raiders and the Minnesota Vikings. Late in the game, a burly Oakland defensive lineman intercepted a screen pass and began rumbling toward the end zone.

Moments later, realizing that he was running with all the speed and grace of a wounded hippo, the lineman wisely lateraled the ball to a speedy teammate. (We don't want to embarrass this guy, so we'll just call him by his number, 48.) Good old 48 had a clear path to the end zone. He should have sprinted in for the score, then gone back to thank the lineman who made the whole thing possible by intercepting the ball.

But no, this is today's NFL, with 40 percent less judgment and class than the old NFL. Flashy 48 deliberately slowed to a trot, looking back at the mammoth Vikings lumbering after him. As the pursuers closed in, 48 turned around and taunted them with the ball, waving it enticingly in front of their faces like a giant oblong cookie.

Then, as he neared the goal line, this not-so-hot dog pranced into the end zone like a cast member from *Riverdance*. This almost made us hurl our chips and dip. Hey, 48 (and everybody like you), it's pre-season. You're supposed to be a professional athlete. Grow up or join the circus.

2. *Speaking of circus, "professional boxing" has become an oxymoron*, just like "free-will offering," "unbiased opinion," and "MTV's *Real World*"—and Don King is the ringmaster. King, whose ideas are as ridiculous and wild as his hair, continues to put together contests whose participants are as mismatched as Lisa Marie Presley and . . . well, pretty much any of her husbands.

King-promoted bouts last about as long as an ice cube on a hot skillet. He usually pits some "up-and-coming contender" against a seasoned boxer who has honed his skills by lifting weights every day and beating up other inmates during his latest incarceration.

Here's another thing we hate about today's boxing: Advertising has made its mark on fighters. Literally. Watch a boxing extravaganza and you'll likely see fighters with the name of a casino or some ad slogan temporarily tattooed to their backs.

You see, the outrageous purses boxers earn aren't enough. Today's pugilist can make an extra few thousand dollars by displaying "Strong enough for a man, but made for a woman" on his sweaty skin.

"I don't see anything wrong with it," we heard a boxer explain in a recent interview. "As long as I'm out there, I might as well be using myself to advertise a product or service."

Allow us to retort, Mr. Pugilist. Yes, you are advertising something, but it's not a product or service. What you are really proclaiming to the world is "I'm a Big Corporate Tool." Why don't you put that on your back for your next fight? (You can use this page to ensure that you don't misspell "Corporate.")

Many players are higher than ever, and we're not talking about their vertical-leaping ability.

---

3. *Pro basketball, football, and baseball are in danger of going to pot.* Literally. Many players are higher than ever, and we're not talking about their vertical-leaping ability. In recent times the Portland Trail Blazers (or is it Jail Blazers?) have garnered so many arrests for pot possession— among other things—that they are thinking of naming Cheech & Chong honorary mascots.

It's time for the NBA, NFL, and MLB to weed out these pot-puff-daddies. Here's the deal, you doobie-blazing 'ballers: If you can't get high on the fact that God blessed you with extraordinary athletic talent that allows you to make millions of dollars, you need help. Use some of that cash to check yourself into Betty Ford or some-place like it and get yourselves level. The only herbs you need to be consuming are those in Kentucky Fried Chicken.

4. Too many teen athletes are forsaking an education for the sake of a game. It's a common story: An eighteen-year-old basketball player hooks up with a sleazy agent with a bad hairpiece and is lured away from an education by prom-ises of multimillion-dollar contracts, adoring female fans, personal trainers, free merchandise, and national TV expo-sure. So the athlete grabs for the brass rim and is instantly transformed into a millionaire. Now he has all the money and adulation that success brings, yet none of the maturity to handle it. That's all our country needs—more ignorant millionaires. (Can we get a witness from laid-off Enron, HP, and WorldCom employees out there?)

Sure, a few of these teen phenoms handle the chal-lenges well and become solid players and solid citizens. But others get injured, fall prey to drugs, or simply don't pan out as players. Do you think the sleazy agents will help them then? You can bet your 15-percent commission that the answer is no. So these glory-grabbers end up in jail, in some minor league that pays its players even less than humor writers (ouch!), or walking along the high-ways, collecting aluminum cans and talking to themselves.

A quick sidebar on this topic: We sympathize with the desire to start making money as soon as possible. Hey, in middle school we both wanted to be lawyers. But there were three problems. First, we didn't understand much about law, only what we'd seen on TV. Second, we weren't smart enough to pass the bar exam—and unlike NBA prospects, we couldn't arrange to have someone else take the test for us. And finally, since we weren't old enough to have a driver's license, our mom would have been required to drive us to court every day, and she said, "No way am I fighting that downtown traffic, boys!"

So, athletes, please stay in school. Or how about working toward your degree and playing basketball at the same time? People balance career and education all the time. Besides, the NBA season doesn't last that long—especially if you play for the Denver Nuggets and have no chance of qualifying for the playoffs.

Thus, in conclusion, here's our encouragement to you high-profile athletes out there: Grow up and be men. (We were going to say "Grow up and be men and women," but when was the last time you heard of a famous female athlete driving drunk, spitting on a fan, abusing her spouse, or brawling with the police?)

We've heard the tired excuse from some of you: "Hey, I didn't choose to be a role model!" Too bad. Some people choose to be role models; others are chosen. You are in the public eye. Kids are watching you. You will be an example to them. How about being a good example instead of a bad one?

Our dad and many other pastors love sports. They'll probably continue to use sports analogies and illustrations in their sermons. It's a tradition as old as the apostle Paul. So please, the next time they talk about an athlete's "arresting performance," let's make it something they glean from the sports pages, not the police report.

THE RICH MAN'S BORROWED CLOTHES
(REMEMBERING RICH MULLINS)

Jedd is making a donut run, so I, Todd, will have to fly solo on this chapter. I'm inspired to write something right now because I'm sitting here listening to a Rich Mullins song—and I'm nowhere near a radio or a stereo. (I'll explain later.)

I first met Rich in the mid-1980s. At the time he sported a crew cut and was billed as a merry and zany songmeister. (The press kit for his debut album included a photo of Rich sporting an impish grin—and a Butterfinger candy bar.) My formal introduction to Rich came at a private luncheon in Nashville. It was just Rich, a few record executives, and a table full of media folk like me.

Many of my colleagues were peppering him with questions and compliments, but Rich wasn't loving the attention. He looked as if he had eaten a tainted chimichanga, and lunch hadn't been served yet.

Sensing the tension at the table, I tried to crack a few jokes. Rich looked at me the way a PETA activist might look at a slaughterhouse worker wearing a full-length mink coat and munching a panda burger.

I left the lunch feeling a bit sorry for Rich. And a bit hurt that I couldn't make him laugh. Or even smile. Still, I liked the guy's music. He wrote and sang like he meant it. His songs went beyond your ears, beyond your intellect. They connected with your soul. His debut album was good, and those that followed were even better. He challenged listeners, "Open your eyes and see / you're on the verge of a miracle." Of his faith in Christ, he proclaimed, "I did not make it / No, it is making me."

In subsequent trips to Nashville, I quit trying so hard to impress Rich with my comic wit and just decided to be myself. And we started to become friends. We talked about all kinds of subjects, and I was struck by his candor. Christian celebrities (a term Rich hated) tend to guard their conversations like watchdogs, especially when talking to someone who works for "the media."

But Rich didn't care. He said what he believed, whether it was on the record, off the record, or about one of his records. Once, when he gave me a ride from the Nashville airport, he said bluntly, "Philosophically, I don't see how you can be a Republican and a Christian. Yet I see so many Christian Republicans who are good people, people I admire."

I told him that only a few days earlier, a pastor I admire had said the same thing—about Democrats. Rich grinned and shook his head. "It's a hard one to figure out, isn't it?" he said.

As the years rolled by and Rich's career began to soar, I tried to stay in touch with him. We played basketball. We ate lots of tepid, rubbery catered food. One time we were

supposed to run together. But Rich forgot to pack his running shoes, and I, in a ridiculous attempt to impress some female publicists from various record companies, loaded up a Nautilus machine with too much weight and messed up my back. We sat around and joked about it, until I laughed too hard and made my back hurt even more.

Despite enjoying many good times with him, I didn't truly bond with Rich until the late '80s, when I met up with him at Mr. Spanky's Formal Wear (or maybe it was Mr. Formal's Spanking-Good Tuxedos) in Nashville. It was April, the season of the Dove Awards (Christian music's answer to the Grammys), and as a member of the Dove's governing body, I was supposed to sit in one of the front rows for the nationally televised awards program.

I mentioned this to my wife on the phone, and she insisted that I not wear my typical T-shirt and blue jeans to a formal awards presentation. She told me lovingly but firmly, "Don't you dare disgrace me and our children by looking like a ragamuffin on TV, okay, idiot?"

So there I was at Mr. Spanky's, studying my reflection in one of the shop's myriad mirrors. I saw an unshaven lanky doofus wearing a triathlon T-shirt peppered with holes. "They provide important ventilation," I explained to my wife every time she tried to throw this shirt away— or use it to strip off furniture polish. The reflection I saw also wore a pair of gray shorts, which were formerly a pair of gray sweatpants. (They had to be downsized after a spirited game of touch football. "Touch" in the sense that Mike Tyson likes to touch his boxing opponents.) Road-ragged running shoes with 587 miles on them completed my ensemble.

I wasn't repulsed by what I saw. It wasn't flashy, but it was comfortable. Back in college, one of my professors had urged me to pattern my wardrobe after a famous celebrity I admired. I had chosen Willie Nelson.

However, while I wasn't ashamed of myself, I was beginning to feel out of place among all the gel-haired music executives prancing and preening in their newly rented penguin suits. Then Rich walked in. A man after my own tailor. He was wearing a T-shirt almost as battered as mine, old shorts, and sandals. And he apparently hadn't shaved for at least three days. My stubble wanted to bow in homage to his.

Rich was followed by his girlfriend. He glanced nervously from me to her, and I knew immediately why she was there. Rich was going to get tuxed, too, and his woman was there to ensure that he got tuxed right.

While a team of Spankettes measured us for our formal wear, Rich and I commiserated about the bizarre American custom in which hapless males pay big money to wear someone else's used clothes. "You'd think somebody should be paying us," Rich noted.

I nodded, adding, "I'm afraid that, after a few hours in this monkey suit, I'll start drinking expensive European bottled water and using words like 'paradigm.'"

After measurements were completed, shoes were fitted, and cummerbunds explained, Rich and I stood side by side, tuxefied.

"Don't you two look smart?" his girlfriend gushed.

Rich and I exchanged glances, and each of us knew what the other was thinking: *We just spent more than a hundred bucks to rent used, goofy-looking clothes for twenty-*

four hours. "Smart" is not the word that pops to mind.

That night we spent a fidgety, itchy three hours in our front-and-center seats. There is simply no way to get comfortable knowing that you are actually wearing something called a cummerbund. After the Doves had all migrated to their rightful owners, Rich and I compared dress-shoe-induced blisters and vowed that henceforth, we would try to enjoy the Doves from backstage, where there was no dress code and one could feast like a Viking on free brownies, Chick-Fil-A chicken, and all the root beer a man cared to guzzle.

We did our best to live up to the pact, although Rich had to opt out during the years his musical genius garnered him award nominations.

The last time I saw Rich in person was October of 1995, when I covered his Colorado Springs concert for *CCM Magazine*. The evening was vintage Rich. Fliers for the event billed it as "An Evening With Rich Mullins and the Ragamuffin Band." I had to smile when I read the words. For much of my life I had been called a ragamuffin, as an insult, and here was Rich Mullins, a respected artist, who chose the name.

---

*T*here is simply no way to get comfortable knowing you are wearing something called a cummerbund.

"What's a ragamuffin?" I heard a young girl ask a

friend before Rich and his band took the stage that night.

She soon got her answer. Rich was about halfway through a sixty-five-city tour, and he and most of his band mates were stricken with the flu. But he was all smiles backstage, complimenting me on my Jars of Clay jacket and saying how much he liked the band. Then Rich and friends put on a three-hour concert/clinic on The Essence of Ragamuffinism.

Here's what we all learned:

1. *Ragamuffins aren't obsessed with pomp and fashion.* Rich performed in a lavender T-shirt and blue jeans. No shoes. No socks. He casually sipped a can of Diet Coke between songs—often between verses.

His attire perfectly reflected the mood of the concert. There were no laser shows, no posturing, no hype.

2. *Ragamuffins share with friends.* In an age when some artists demand—literally—how much of the spotlight should shine on them, Rich proved to be an anomaly. He graciously shared the stage with Carolyn Arends and his other special guest, Ashley Cleveland. Both women did opening sets, came back to showcase more of their considerable talents near the end of the show, then joined Rich for a three-song encore.

Rich also took time to acknowledge his crack six-piece band and trio of backing vocalists. He didn't roar, "Everybody in the house—let's give it up for Beaker!" but instead talked about his relationships with Beaker and other members of the team.

Mullins urged the audience to share, as well—by supporting The Jesus Way project, an International Bible

Society effort to provide a culturally relevant version of the Scriptures to Native Americans. (Only two percent of Native Americans claim to be Christians.) Rich was more than a poster boy for this effort. He was living and teaching music on a Navajo reservation at the time.

3. *Ragamuffins deliver the goods.* Despite its casualness—or perhaps because of it—the concert itself was first-rate. Rich, who was creeping up on age forty, seemed more at ease with his audience than ever before. He sang with confidence and power—despite the flu—mixing songs from his new album with favored classics like "Hold Me, Jesus."

Throughout the evening Rich invited the audience to participate on many songs by singing along, shaking their car keys, even dancing. And how this arena full of mostly white evangelicals did dance—just like a bunch of mostly white evangelicals. Some looked like they were trying to stamp out small brushfires. Others . . . well, imagine people standing board-stiff in a windstorm, and you'll get the idea. "You people don't get to dance much, do you?" Rich observed.

Rich, Ashley Cleveland, and Carolyn Arends closed the show with three hymns, leaving the stage as the audience completed the Doxology.

As they praised God, "from Whom all blessings flow," all in the crowd no doubt realized that those blessings can spring from many sources, including an ailing pack of Ragamuffins with a shoeless leader.

During the next two years I changed careers and wasn't able to be a regular at music-industry events. I missed my "Rich times," but I still kept up with him as best I could. I read articles about him. We served as columnists for the same magazine. Mostly, though, I stayed in touch with him through his music. His songs became part of my inner soundtrack, my sonic landscape. They reminded me of God's grace and encouraged me to strive for the passionate, nothing-held-back kind of faith that Rich had.

On a November day in 1997, I got a phone call from a friend at Compassion International, for whom Rich served as a faithful spokesperson. An auto accident had killed him. At first I cried. Then I grabbed one of his albums and just sat back and listened. The songs were like letters of hope and encouragement from an old friend. The kind you never tire of reading. The kind that stick in your head and your heart long after the music stops playing.

That's why on nights like tonight, even with no CD player or radio around, I still hear you, Rich Mullins.

12

Longing to Be Part of the Inn Crowd,
Part 1

One of the benefits of being comedian/speaker types is the travel it provides. We get to meet people from all over the country, see famous landmarks (such as Kansas's three-story concrete prairie dog), and stay in cool hotels.

We love hotels. We love the little bars of soap, because when you use them, it makes your muscles seem huge by comparison. We love it that the toilets have been SANITIZED FOR OUR PROTECTION. That makes us feel special. Also, we love room service. Not to mention cable TV, especially ESPN, which we don't get to watch very much at home because of that darned SpongeBob SquarePants.

That's why we look forward to staying in Motel _____ (fill in the number of your choice) when we are on a speaking junket.

Unfortunately, sometimes the church, civic organization, or electrolysis clinic that sponsors us wants us to stay at one of its members' homes. Sure, this seems like a good idea on the surface. It saves money. It provides us home cookin' while we are away from our own abodes. And it avoids that valet parking nonsense.

In reality, however, staying at someone's house is fraught with more pitfalls than a prairie dog town. You see, we've simply had too many stays like the one at the Schneider home. It seems like it was just last month. Oh yeah, it *was* just last month.

We drove from Colorado through a desolate part of New Mexico, known as "New Mexico." We arrived at the Schneider place tired, numb-bunned, and hungry. (To save money, we agreed to subsist only on Wrigley's Spearmint gum and two bottles of strawberry Yoo-Hoo.)

From the outside, Casa de Schneider seemed harmless, if a bit unusual. The home was adobe, painted electric lime green. A hand-lettered sign on the front door proclaimed, AS FOR ME AND MY HOUSE, WE WILL SERVE THE LORD. Unfortunately, due to the crudeness of the hand-lettering, it looked more like AS FOR ME AND MY HORSE, WE WILL SEVER THE LARD.

We knocked on the door (yes, we both knocked, to the tune of "The William Tell Overture") and were met by a pear-shaped, anxious woman with glasses the size of small TV sets. Her pinkish-blond hair was pulled back so severely from her forehead that she resembled a test pilot experiencing a G force of 6.5.

"Hello!" she called, as if yelling to us from across the Ponderosa. "You must be the Haffner boys!"

"Hafer," Jedd corrected.

"Yes, indeedy-doo!" said Mrs. Schneider. "Now, which one of you is Tom, and which one is Jeff?"

"It doesn't really matter," Jedd answered quietly.

"Oh! Ha! Now, is that one of your jokes, you silly boy?"

Before we had a chance to answer, our hostess urged us into the adobe abode.

"Just have a seat anywhere," she told us cheerfully.

Jedd picked a rust-colored ottoman. Todd selected a sturdy, straight-backed wooden chair that looked as if it weighed four hundred pounds.

"Oh, now look what you've done," Mrs. Schneider fretted at Todd. "You've picked the most uncomfortable chair in the house!"

"Well, I have a bad back. . . ." he began.

"He likes hard chairs," Jedd offered.

"I won't hear of it!" Mrs. S countered. "It makes me squirm just to look at him."

With that, she grabbed Todd by the wrist and flung him into a beanbag chair that engulfed him like a hungry taupe marshmallow.

While Todd battled to free himself from the evil soft chair, our hostess announced, "Now that you are comfortable, you simply must meet Phoebe!"

We smiled. We love to meet our hosts' children. Kids seem to enjoy our brand of humor most—and they usually know where the cookies are stashed.

Mrs. S smacked her hands together three times and snapped, "Phoebe! In!"

We frowned. We don't favor overly regimented parenting techniques. Then Phoebe bounded into the room on all fours, her long pink tongue dangling from her cavernous mouth.

You probably figured it out two paragraphs ago:

Phoebe was a dog. (Still is, to the best of our knowledge.) And we're not talking some little teacup poodle or Shih Tzu. We're talking a camel-sized mutt who puts the Great in Great Dane. Phoebe looked us over for a moment; then she barked once and attacked Jedd with the speed and ferocity of a Mongol warrior.

---

*J*edd screamed as Phoebe's teeth punctured his ankle.

Mrs. S smiled at Jedd. "Don't mind Phoebe," she called as she went into the kitchen. "She's just a pup."

Meanwhile, Phoebe, growling like an enraged she-bear, had her four-inch puppy canines embedded in Jedd's new $150 basketball shoes.

Mrs. S returned from the kitchen as Phoebe began to twist her massive neck from side to side, nearly dislocating Jedd's hip. "Oh, Phoebe," Mrs. S cooed, "you be a sweet girl."

Phoebe continued to maul.

"How do you boys like your coffee?" Mrs. S asked cheerfully.

"Black," Todd said.

"Aieeee! Black!" Jedd screamed as Phoebe's teeth punctured his ankle.

Mrs. S's perma-smile drooped slightly. "Well, I made both of yours with cream and sugar. You probably just don't like cream and sugar because you get that awful city-store-bought stuff. This is REAL cream, from Mrs. Hampstead up the road."

We both prayed silently that Mrs. Hampstead owned a cow.

"And the sugar," she continued, "is real cane sugar given to us by a missionary named Leilani Kai-Luau, who spoke at our church two years ago and told the parable of the talents with a hula dance!"

At that moment the Schneiders' eight-year-old daughter, Naomi, came in the front door. Phoebe released her grip on Jedd and charged after Naomi. Naomi screamed and bolted up the stairs, Phoebe snapping her foam-flecked jaws in heated pursuit.

"Naomi," Mrs. S chuckled, "you quit teasing poor Phoebe."

Naomi didn't answer. We saw her make it to her bedroom, dash inside, and slam the door. Phoebe launched herself against the door, but it held. Phoebe bounced off the door and slumped to the floor, barked once, then laid her head on her forepaws and fell asleep.

Jedd studied the bite marks on his ankle for a few moments, then glanced at his watch. "Hey," he said, "it's six o'clock. Time for SportsCenter!"

"Da-da-da! Da-da-DA!" we sang in unison the closing bars of the SportsCenter theme song.

"Oh, piffle," Mrs. S said with disgust. "Sports are so silly. So is all of TV. That's why last month I took my pinking shears and cut our cable right in two. And you know what? We haven't missed those dumb old TV shows one bit."

"Piffle?" Jedd said weakly.

"But don't you worry, boys," Mrs. S assured. "We do have a VCR. Of course, we don't use it for worldly entertainment purposes. But we do have the complete set of my husband, Clem's, sermons on the minor prophets. You know, that Obadiah was a fascinating man of God. Let me put the first tape in right now. We can watch it together!"

She dragged a cardboard box the size of a bathtub from the living room closet and selected a tape. "The sound's a little bad, so I'll have to turn it up so you can hear it," she said.

"Jedd," Todd whispered, "maybe later we can go out to a pizza shop where they have a TV and . . ."

"'IF GRAPE PICKERS CAME TO YOU, WOULD THEY NOT LEAVE A FEW GRAPES?' LET US EXAMINE THIS QUESTION, OKEY-DOKEY?"

Clem's loud and distorted voice filled the room and probably the neighborhood. The volume was so high that it felt like Clem was inside our skulls, yelling through a bullhorn.

As we winced from the pain, we studied the plump man, wearing overalls and a porkpie hat, smiling at us from the twenty-four-inch black-and-white TV set.

"CLEM IS A GREAT MAN OF GOD!" Mrs. S screamed, her voice escalating to Clem-like decibel levels.

"Could you add some arsenic to my coffee so that I might die right now?" Jedd inquired.

"HUH?" Mrs. S asked with a smile.

Jedd just grimaced and pulled a small notebook from his back pocket. (A comic always carries a notebook; you never know when inspiration will strike.)

"I JUST THOUGHT OF A GREAT BIT!" Jedd announced.

"AND JUST WHAT DO YOU THINK YOU'RE DOING, YOUNG MAN?" Mrs. S asked in mock anger. "I READ IN A MAGAZINE THAT YOU BOYS ARE WORKAHOLICS. WELL, NOT IN MY HOUSE! THERE WILL BE NO WRITING. I WANT YOU TO RELAX FOR THE NEXT TWO DAYS, YOU NAUGHTY BOYS. YOU SAVE YOUR ENERGY FOR THE DEDICATION SPEECH FOR THE KICKIN' FOR CHRIST KUNG-FU SCHOOL, YOU HEAR ME?"

"But . . ." Jedd offered weakly.

"YOU ARE OUR GUESTS HERE. NOT ONE JOT NOR TITTLE WILL YOU WRITE WHILE YOU ARE HERE IN THE BOSOM OF OUR HOUSEHOLD!"

"Tittle," Jedd said absently, looking as if he'd just bitten into a tainted fish taco. Then, to calm his nerves, he dipped his hand into his right front pocket and removed a roll of Mentos (the Freshmaker!).

Suddenly Mrs. S's right hand shot out like a rattlesnake with liver spots and snatched the Mentos from Jedd's hand.

"Uh-uh-uh!" she scolded, "you give those to me. We can't have our guests providing their own mints. Besides, how do you know that Mister Mentos loves the Lord? You don't want to snack on unholy victuals, do you? Let me go get my purse."

She disappeared from the room, returning moments later with a black purse the size of a corn-fattened woodchuck. "Try one of these," she said, producing a black plastic cylindrical tube. "They're Zin-Zins!"

She shook a few hard pea-colored octagons into Jedd's hand. "You'll find these much tastier than your old worldly mints," she promised. "And they promote healthy bowel functioning!"

"I'll try them later," Jedd said.

"Oh, piffle! You simply must try them right now, Jeff. You might as well get used to them. We have them after every meal—and after morning devotions."

Looking defeated, Jedd reluctantly sampled a few Zin-Zins. Then, graciously, he offered to share a few with his big brother.

"They taste like rancid fire ants," Jedd whispered.

"Dipped in motor oil," Todd added.

"What's that, boys?" Mrs. S queried.

"Where's your bathroom?" Jedd said, desperation creeping into his voice.

While Mrs. S led Jedd to the facilities, Todd crawled through his window of opportunity and spat out his vile Zin-Zins in a fake ficus tree.

Several minutes later we found ourselves in our sleeping room, furnished with two single beds that must have been custom-built for a pair of *The Wizard of* Oz Munchkins. We sat on our respective mini-beds and marveled at all that had transpired. We wondered what would happen when we met Clem in person. And we wondered if we would ever get a chance to work on the book you're reading now. We had no idea what was in store for us during our remaining time at Casa de Schneider. Conflict. Disappointment. Bewilderment. Indigestion. And wrought iron. Lots and lots of wrought iron. But that is another chapter. In fact, it's the next chapter. . . .

13

LONGING TO BE PART OF THE INN CROWD,
PART 2

"HELLO, BOYS!" Clem Schneider yelled as he entered our room without knocking. We quickly realized that he had only one volume: LOUD.

"I THOUGHT YOU FELLERS WOULD LIKE TO SEE MY WROUGHT-IRON GATE OUT FRONT. YOU KNOW, I HELPED WROUGHT SOME OF THE IRON MYSELF! ME AND THE MISSUS WILL BE GONE MOST OF TOMORROW, AND I FIGURED YOU'D ENJOY THE FENCE MORE IF YOU KNEW SOME OF ITS BACKGROUND. OF COURSE, TO FULLY APPRE-CIATE IT, YOU SHOULD COME BACK IN THE SPRING, AFTER I DO THE MAJOR POLISHING."

"We're usually swamped at springtime," Jedd noted.

As for the forty-five-minute tour of the fence, we don't remember much. But we do recall that Clem used the phrase METALLURGIC MARVEL twenty-eight times. He concluded his presentation by lowering his voice (only slightly) and saying, "YOU KNOW, FELLERS, WHEN I SEE THE STRENGTH AND DIGNITY OF

MY WROUGHT-IRON FENCE, IT BREAKS MY HEART THAT SOME PEOPLE LOWER THEIR STANDARDS AND GO WITH CHAIN LINK."

He dabbed at the corners of his eyes with a red-checkered hanky. "IT JUST AIN'T RIGHT. NO SIREE BOB-DINKUM. IT JUST AIN'T RIGHT."

"Indeed," Jedd agreed quietly.

Later that evening, safe within the wrought-iron encircled fortress, we dined with the Schneiders. We sat down at the dinner table with a sense of hope, certain that our stay had hit its nadir with the over-wrought iron saga.

Then came the meal: lots of tough meat and droopy vegetables under an array of heavy sauces. We searched in vain for Phoebe the Killer Dog, hoping to unload some of our victuals on her, but she would not come within twenty feet of the dining room table.

"There is nothing like a home-cooked meal to fill you up, is there, boys?" Mrs. S asked us.

"Right you are," Todd said. "This meal will certainly fill us up."

"If we can keep it down," Jedd whispered.

"MOMMA-BIRD," Clem queried his wife, "ARE YOU GONNA EAT ALL YOUR GRISTLE?"

"Well, yes I am, you old gristle-poacher! You just mind your own gristle!"

"Good advice for all of us," Jedd said.

"Amen, Brother Jedd," Naomi said.

Everyone at the table nodded in solemn agreement.

At this point, Clem decided to change the subject. But he took our conversation down a twisty, dangerous road. The journey began with a seemingly innocent question:

Clem: "HOW DID YOU TWO LEARN TO BE FUNNY? DO THEY HAVE FUNNY-BOY CLASSES AT THEM UNIVERSITIES AND SUCH?"

"Any-hoo, when you fellers write one of them jokes, do you come up with the punch line first? Or all the boring stuff that goes before it?"

Todd: "We have little formal training. Mainly we watch Jay Leno and steal his jokes. Ha-ha-ha!"

Clem: "LENO, EH? IS THAT ARABIAN?"

Mrs. S: "Stealing? That doesn't sound ethical to me, boys. Remember, WWJD?!"

Todd: "Oh, please let me clarify: I was just joking."

Clem: "WHO IS JAY LENO? IS HE SAVED? DOES HE KNOW OUR LORD JESUS PERSONALLY?"

Mrs. S: "Of course not, dear. He's from Hollywood."

Clem: "ANY-HOO, WHEN YOU FELLERS WRITE ONE OF THEM JOKES, DO YOU COME UP WITH THE PUNCH LINE FIRST? OR ALL THE BORING STUFF THAT GOES BEFORE IT?"

Jedd: "Sometimes one way; sometimes the other."

Clem: "THAT'S VERY INTERESTING, JEB."

Naomi: "Daddy—how is that interesting? It seems kind of a wishy-washy answer to me."

Mrs. S: "Naomi, you shush up and eat your corn pone."

Clem: "SO, DO YOU BOYS HAVE REAL JOBS BESIDES THE FUNNY-BOY STUFF AND WHATNOT?"

Todd: "Well, we each have two jobs, but comedy pays about half the bills for each of us."

Clem: "YOU MEAN TO TELL ME THERE'S GOOD MONEY IN BEING SILLY AND SUCH?"

Jedd: "We do all right."

Clem: "IS THAT SO? WHAT DID YOU EACH NET LAST YEAR? AFTER 'RENDERING UNTO CAESAR'?"

Jedd: "Say, is there any more of that corn pone left?"

Clem: "YOU KNOW, MOMMA-BIRD, THESE HAFFNER BOYS SURE DID ADORE MY WROUGHT-IRON FENCE."

Mrs. S: "Well, of course they did. But, boys, you really must come in the spring when Clem polishes it up real nice."

Todd and Jedd (in unison): "We're simply slammed in the spring."

Mrs. S: "How about the fall, then? The fence still looks right proud come autumn."

Todd and Jedd (still unisonic): "We've no free time at all in the fall."

Naomi (rolling up pant leg): "Hey, guys, Phoebe bit me on the calf last week. Does this look infected to you? I don't think bites are supposed to ooze this much, do you?"

Mrs. S: "Now, you hush, Naomi! We don't want these Hatter boys thinking badly of poor Phoebe. You just sop up the rest of your gravy with that last bit of corn pone, and we'll apply some Balm o' Gilead or some cow-udder salve to your little doggie nip later."

Clem: "YOU KNOW, I'VE BEEN A-WATCHING YOU FELLERS EAT. YOU AIN'T DONE TOO WELL ON YOUR VEGGIES AND MEATS— NOT EVEN MOMMA-BIRD'S FAMOUS POS- SUM. BUT YOU'VE HAD TWO HELPINGS APIECE OF THE CORN PONE. IF I DIDN'T KNOW BETTER, I'D SAY YOU HEAVILY FAVOR THE CORN PONE. AM I RIGHT OR AM I RIGHT?"

Jedd: "There's just no fooling you, Clem."

Todd: "You know, we both love corn, and we both love pone. So this is really a double treat for us!"

Mrs. S (stifling a giggle): "Make that a triple treat, right, Clem?"

Clem: "DON'T YOU KNOW IT, MOMMA-BIRD!"

Jedd: "Triple treat?"

Mrs. S: "That's right, Jeff! I always stir two cups of Metamucil into all of my baked goods—corn pone, hoecakes, cheese grits, you name it. A clean colon is a happy colon!"

With that, we retreated to our room to await the gas- tric plague we feared would strike us presently. We were playing Rock, Paper, Scissors to see who would get to use the bathroom first when we heard a knock at the door.

"Knock-knock!" Mrs. S said loudly, apparently trans- lating in case we were knocking-impaired. "I brought you some extra blankets in case you're not warm enough."

"We're as warm as toast," Jedd called from our side of the door.

"Oh my, but I'm afraid you're not, boys. You don't know what it's like to live where we have real winters."

"We're from Colorado," Jedd pointed out.

Todd whispered, "Lock the door, or she's going to come in and feel our noses."

Mrs. S said she would leave the blankets at our door, just in case, but she needn't have worried. We were plenty warm that night. Particularly so at 11:48, when the Corn 'n' Metamucil Pone kicked in. Jedd made it to the bathroom first. As for his older brother, we don't wish to be indelicate, so let's just say that he was forced to run outside, and, well, the Schneiders have a lilac bush that will likely never bloom again.

We were awakened the following morning by the sound of Mrs. S hollering at someone. We crept from our room, wondering if Naomi was being reprimanded for teasing the killer dog again.

We found Mrs. S on the phone in the kitchen, scolding someone with gusto: "Now, you see here, you entertainment-industry reprobate. This is the third time you have called this morning, interrupting my time of hot beverage and devotions, I might add. So you had best listen up this time: Tom and Jess Haffner are not interested in auditioning for any show featuring Mister Letter-Person, or whatever his name is!"

We looked at each other in horror.

"You are not hearing me, little missy," Mrs. S continued. "Won't you leave these poor boys alone?! They have no interest in working with any Letter-Person. I'm sure they have nothing against educational TV, but Mister Letter-Person will just have to find someone else to teach his young viewers their ABC's. Huh? What's that?"

Mrs. S turned to us. "Oh, you boys won't believe what this woman is asking now.

"No, no, no—not in a million years—which is like unto only a day to our Lord—will these nice boys consider performing in Las Vegas. Why, Las Vegas is the very belly of Hades itself. You know what my darling Clem calls it? Lost Wages! Isn't he clever? Anyway, these fine young men are not interested in performing in such a den of iniquity. What's that . . . Well, I'm sorry that Carrot Top has the flu, but that's not my problem, my unregenerate friend! And maybe if Mr. Carrot Top ate more fiber, he wouldn't have fallen ill in the first place."

With that, Mrs. S hung up the phone like Shaquille O'Neal dunks a basketball. "Well," she said proudly, "I fixed her little red wagon."

"Whose little red wagon?" Jedd asked tentatively.

"Oh, it was Tiffany or Stacey or Jade or something like that. Not a good solid biblical name like Sarah or Rachel or Dorcas. At any rate, she was trying to lead you into all sorts of dens of iniquities, all for the lure of the almighty mammon."

"How much mammon was she talking about?" Todd asked.

"Oh, piffle on money! You boys are doing just fine, I can tell. You're both a little gangly, but other than that you seem in good health."

"You said something about Mister Letter-Person," Jedd began. "Are you sure it wasn't Letterman?"

Mrs. S snorted. "Letterman, Letterhead, Leadbetter, Bedwetter, Wool Sweater, Double-Header, Sharp Cheddar—what's the difference? You boys don't need to be any part of some late-night TV tomfoolery."

Mrs. S paused and took a deep sip from a large mug. "Ahh, Postum!" she said with a smile. "Anyway, I am glad I was finally able to get rid of Tiffany or Ashley or Ione or whatever her name was. She was almost as irksome as that man from that network who called for you last night."

"Network?" Jedd sighed, leaning on a crate of Clem's videos for support. "Which one? ABC, NBC, HBO, CBS, the WB?"

Mrs. S chewed her bottom lip thoughtfully. "Hmm. A couple of those sound familiar. I'm pretty sure there was a B involved. But anyway, who cares about an appearance in a TV special? What's so special about TV, anyway? To me, it's not special unless Clem is on it!"

We stared at each other in disbelief. Who would have thought that—just when fate finally tossed us the chance of a lifetime—a corn-pone-packin' mama would intercept it and run the other way for a touchdown?

Later that evening, after our gig at the Kickin' for Christ Kung-Fu School, we sat in our room, packing. We discussed playing a little prank on Mrs. S, just as we do when a hotel annoys or mistreats us. But it's not that easy to exact good-natured revenge against a home. You can't put red food coloring in the swimming pool. You can't leave the Gideon Bible open to a passage describing destruction and judgment—along with a note reading, THIS MEANS YOU, YOU MOTEL 6 HEATHENS!

Sure, we could have stolen some towels, but they all smelled of Great Dane.

So we decided to somberly shake the corn pone off our sandals and leave quietly. As we exited the Schneider house, Mrs. S pleaded with us, "Are you sure you must leave tonight? There are lots of drunken heathens in foreign cars on the road at this time."

"Yes, we really must be going," Jedd said. "We have to get back home in time to open for a mime troupe at a public-park amphitheater."

"Well, go ye then if you must. *Vaya con Dios, amigos!*"

"Chili con carne!" Todd replied.

"Don't blaspheme, Ted," Mrs. S reprimanded. Then she handed us a large brown grocery bag with grease spots around its base. "Well, since you won't be here for my famous corn-pone pancakes tomorrow morning, here is the next best thing: M&M&M cookies!"

"Let me guess," Jedd said. "M&Ms and Metamucil?"

"Oh, you are so smart, Jeff!" She leaned in and whispered to him, "I bet you won't have to be in comedy very long, not like your poor oafish big brother, bless his heart."

We waved goodbye to Mrs. Schneider and asked that she give Clem, Naomi, and Phoebe a holy good-night kiss for us. Jedd banged his knee on the wrought-iron gate as we exited the yard, but he was too tired to say ouch—or even to bruise.

As we merged onto the interstate, Jedd said, "Let's just hope that if fortune ever tries to smile on us again, Mrs. Schneider won't be there to punch it in the mouth."

"Indeed," Todd said.

After four hours of driving, we became hungry.

Knowing that we had only enough money for gas, we war-ily opened the bag of M&M&M cookies.

"Well," Todd reasoned, "it's probably better than starving."

Jedd nodded, plucked a snack from the sack, and took a bite. A puzzled expression crept across his face. "Uh-oh," he said. "There must have been some mix-up back at the Schneider place. These aren't cookies. Hmmm. I think they're Phoebe's dog biscuits."

This revelation was a relief to both of us. We quickly devoured half the bag.

"Look at it this way," Jedd said, waving a half-eaten biscuit for emphasis, "this is the first thing about the whole trip that's worked out better for us. Now we won't have to hit as many rest stops, and just think of all the tartar we'll scrape off our teeth!"

With that, we both stuck our heads out the window, opened our mouths, and enjoyed the ride.

THE 2-FOR-1 HAIRCUT

A few months ago we loaded up Jedd's Geo GL (which we think stands for Gullible Losers) and headed for our sister church up in North Dakota, the Church of the Frozen Tundra. This isn't its real name, of course, but we gave it this moniker after our first couple of visits there because (1) North Dakota has tundra, and (2) much of said tundra is frozen (as are many other things in North Dakota).

We always look forward to visiting COFT and speaking to the congregation there. They seem to like us, probably because they have to put up with us only once or twice a year. Also, North Dakota is cool. Its capital is Bismarck, making it the only state in the Union with a capital named after a pastry.

As we drove, we discussed topics we might share with our brethren and sistren—and the jokes we might use. (In past visits, we found we could earn robust laughter by making fun of South Dakota.)

We pulled into a truck stop near Minot to get a snack.

As we strolled to the entrance, we looked inside the establishment, which was creatively named Al's Truck Stop, and noticed two scraggly strangers inside.

"Look at those guys," Todd commented. "Haven't they heard of that great invention, the comb?"

"I don't even know if one could pull a comb through those unruly mops," Jedd noted. "When was the last time those guys got a haircut, the Carter Administration?"

"Maybe they're Nazirites," Todd offered. "Like Samson."

"I doubt it," Jedd countered. "Look at how gangly they are. They aren't strong like Samson. Delilah could whup the both of them."

"You're probably right," Todd said. "Hey, look, Jedd, one of those scrawny dudes has a Broncos jacket just like yours."

"And one of them is wearing tired old gray Kmart sweats like yours."

That's when it hit us like a big North Dakota snowball. We had met the ragamuffins, and they were us (or is it "we were they"?). We were seeing our own unkempt reflections in the truck-stop window.

"Does our hair really look that bad?" Jedd asked rhetorically.

"I'm afraid so. Truck-stop windows don't lie."

At this point we did some mental retracing and deduced that we hadn't received haircuts in about four months, when we were scheduled to be on a local TV show. (We ended up getting bumped in favor of a guy who bought a half-eaten sandwich on eBay for six hundred dollars. The other half of the sandwich had been eaten by Celine Dion, or maybe it was Deion Sanders, or perhaps Dionne Warwick. It could have been Dion of Dion & the Belmonts. In any case, the discarded food of any of those celebrities was apparently more interesting than the Brothers Hafer.)

Anyway, our heads now looked like mop tops. And not fashionable mop tops like those of the Beatles. Ours were more like stringy, unruly mops that are used to clean prison rest rooms. We knew we could not face the members of our sister church like this. It would be a poor way to represent our home church. It would show a lack of moral character. Besides, the North Dakota teens would make fun of us.

As we entered downtown Minot we strained our eyes, looking for someplace that would bring order to the chaos atop our heads—for under ten bucks, if possible. We saw a couple of high-end salons, Shear Excellence and some other fancy-looking French-looking place called Tressed to Kill (or maybe it was Turn Your Head and Coif). We knew these businesses were for people beyond our social strata and income level. (You have to beware any time you see a hair salon with a sign noting FINANCING AVAILABLE.)

We were growing desperate when we saw Kustom Kutz. We smiled at each other. Places that don't know how to spell are typically quite economical. Beyond economical, in this case. As we pulled into the KK parking lot, we saw a hand-lettered sign in the window. It read, WEEKEND SPECIAL: 2-FOR-1 HAIRCUTZ!

Twenty-two minutes later, we walked through piles of our own hair to the Kustom Kutz exit, feeling lighter in

spirit and lighter in the head, if you know what we mean.

However, as we headed to our car, we began to eye each other suspiciously. All this suspicious eyeing provoked the following exchange:

Todd: "Is something wrong?"

Jedd: "In what way?"

Todd: "Well, you are looking at me funny."

Jedd: "I was just looking at you that way because you are looking at *me* funny."

Todd: "Yeah . . ."

Jedd: "So, why are you doing that?"

Todd: "You first. Why are you looking at me?"

Jedd: "It's just that . . ."

Todd: "Yes?"

Jedd: "Dude, you look like a doofus."

Todd: "I'm just the way God made me, bro. And God doesn't make junk."

Jedd: "That's not what I mean. I mean your hair. Your haircut makes you look like a doofus."

Todd: "Well, so does yours!"

Jedd: "Oh, that's great! Get all defensive, why don't you? You're the older brother. You're supposed to be the mature one."

Todd: "No, I'm not being defensive. You do indeed have a problem with your hair. It looks like somebody turned a hungry badger loose on your head."

Jedd: "Are you serious? That is the same thing I was thinking about you! Only I was going to say enraged ferret instead of hungry badger."

Todd: "Well, six of one . . ."

Jedd: "Didn't you notice how your Kustom Kutz

stylist was mangling your hair? Didn't you look in the mirror?"

"You do indeed have a problem with your hair. It looks like somebody turned a hungry badger loose on your head."

Todd: "Well, no. I was too busy watching your Kustom Kutz stylist do a weed-whacker number on you. Besides, your lady looked like Alice from *The Brady Bunch*. So I was kinda distracted by that. But hey, why weren't you minding *your* appearance?"

Jedd: "For the same reason as yours. Only your stylist looked like Sam the Butcher from *The Brady Bunch*."

Todd: "She did?"

Jedd: "She did indeed."

We reached our car, we studied our reflections in its window, and we panicked. Then we looked at our watches and panicked even more. We had precisely twenty-eight minutes before we were due to entertain and edify a church auditorium full of eager North Dakotans.

Now, you might think that a couple of funny-boys could squeeze gallons of laughter out of a bad-haircut saga like this. But these haircuts weren't bad-funny. They were bad-ghastly. They were prison-camp bad and Pauly Shore unfunny.

We knew that we could not face the believers of COFT in this state. So, following the urging of that wise man Carrot Top, we dialed down the center of a pay phone and called our friend G-Dawg in Los Angeles. He's in the entertainment industry, he's cool, he's unflappable, and he's one of the few people in the country who will accept a collect call from the Brothers Hafer.

We explained our dilemma, both yakking into the phone at the same time. After we finished kvetching, he paused a few moments. Then, in a soothing, measured tone, he said, "Dudes, I have the solution. All you have to do is shave your heads."

We protested furiously. We told G-Dawg we would feel naked without our hair. We told him we feared that if we relinquished our locks, they might never grow back. We told him it would be a hot winter in North Dakota before we would ever shave our heads.

He let us vent. Then he said, "I understand your reservations. But shaved heads are in. Look at Michael Jordan. Look at Bruce Willis. Look at Charles Barkley. Look at Sinead O'Connor."

"Sinead O'Connor?!" we screamed in unison.

"Okay, okay," G-Dawg said. "Don't look at her. But do look at the other guys. They look smooth. They look confident. They save money on shampoo. Power-bald, dudes—it's the look of the future."

The call ended. We knew Mr. Dawg was right. No hair at all had to be better than the hair we were sporting. Besides, the whole Jordan/Willis/Barkley thing was working on us. On the way to the drugstore to purchase a couple of heavy-duty Bic shavers, we took turns naming more cool bald icons: Savalas, Picasso, Connery, Moby (the musician, not the whale).

We zipped into a YMCA and stood before a wall of mirrors, where we proceeded to free our respective noggins of the atrocious 2-for-1 hair butchering. We smiled as we thought of our friend's wise counsel. We wondered whom we would resemble most when we were done— basketball stars or movie action heroes?

We toweled remnant patches of shaving cream off our domes and gazed eagerly at our reflections.

We looked like two scrawny sons of Uncle Fester.

Some people look cool bald. But those people have symmetrically shaped heads that have seen the light of the sun. Our heads looked like hard-boiled eggs that had been peeled, then beaten with a small ball peen hammer.

The congregation at COFT stared at us that evening with looks of shock and pity. It was especially embarrassing to be up there not only bald but with heads dotted with tiny pieces of blood-stained toilet paper.

The whole thing was excruciatingly uncomfortable, but we did get a record-size love offering.

We drove out of Minot that evening. (We didn't get the usual invitation to stay overnight with one of the church families. We learned later that most of them were afraid we would give their children—or their pets—nightmares.) We left filled with embarrassment and despair. Embarrassment over the pasty-domed spectacles we had made of ourselves. Despair over the prospect of having to do gig after gig with our new maimed Uncle Fester look.

How long will it take for our hair to grow back? we wondered. More importantly, how long would it take for our dignity to grow back?

As we neared the North Dakota state line, God must have decided to smile on us or at least wink at us. Because on a large sign outside a gift shop/gas station, we read the words that would cover our present humiliation and protect us from the potential rogue barbarian shops we might encounter in the future. The sign proclaimed: WEEKEND SPECIAL: 2-FOR-1 BASEBALL KAPZ!

Making the Grad

A few years ago, on Promotion Sunday, Cindy, our church's aged Sunday school superintendent, corralled us in the foyer. "You've got to help me, boys," she pleaded. "We booked a special guest entertainer to minister to our high-school seniors and encourage them as they move out into the real world, as it were. But . . ."

"Let me guess," Jedd said. "The Christian mime canceled on you."

Cindy's wrinkly face flushed. "Well, yes, Mr. Smarty-Pants, if you must know. She called earlier in the week and said that her new face paint was giving her a rash and she might not be able to make it. But we didn't hear from her for two days, and then I started calling her answering machine. I have left at least half a dozen messages for her, but she's never returned a one of them."

"So," Todd said, "what you're saying is that a mime is giving you the silent treatment. Hmm."

"Oh, horsefeathers. You're as bad as your little brother. Now, are you two going to help us out by doing one of your lightweight-funny-boy routines, or do I need to call Zeke the janitor and see if he still remembers how to juggle?"

"Don't fret, Original Cindy," Jedd said. "We're here for you."

"Thank you, boys," she said. "But please don't call me Original Cindy. It sounds kinda naughty and it makes me feel old. I'm eighty-six, but I'm sure I'm not the first-ever Cindy! Besides, I work hard around here—have been for fifty-one years. Don't know what this church would do without me, to be frank."

"We don't want you to be Frank," Todd replied. "We need you to be Cindy."

"That's right," Jedd agreed. "Let him who is without Cindy cast a stone upon his foot, for—"

"Oh, land o' Goshen," Cindy shouted, "will you two quit making bad jokes at my expense and get downstairs and inspire our youth, for cryin' out loud?"

And so a tradition was born. Our first commencement address went surprisingly well. In fact, at the risk of being boastful, we must point out that not one of the twenty-nine teens we spoke to that day has been arrested or gone on welfare. (And today, only five years later, two from that group are already assistant managers, at Pizza Hut and Meineke Mufflers, respectively.)

Because of the success of our first commencement foray, we are invited back every year. Sure, some in the congregation have argued that "our precious teens deserve advice from someone more successful than the Hafer yay-hoos," but our supporters are quick to point out two key factors that make us the best choice.

1. We are always available, and we work for free.
2. As Gator the Youth Director points out, "Those Hafer bros are living proof that you don't have to be talented—or all that good-looking—to achieve at least a modicum of success in life."

We believe that today's teens are the people we will depend on to keep the good ship Social Security afloat once we reach retirement age.

Thus, we look forward to every spring. We believe that today's teens are tomorrow's leaders—and the people we will depend on to keep the good ship Social Security afloat once we reach retirement age.

So, as each annual Promotion Sunday draws nigh, we feverishly peruse the Bible, old Dear Abby columns, and the backs of cereal boxes for wise advice that we might pass on to our young audiences. Our yearly address has become known as The Divine 29. Remember, there were twenty-nine students in that first audience of ours, so we decided to pass on one piece of advice, one golden nugget of wisdom, in honor of each person present.

In years since, we have followed the same formula because (1) we believe in tradition, and (2) we feel the number 29 gets short shrift on most lists. It's always top-10 this, top-20 that. Baskin & Robbins could have stopped at 29 flavors. But no, they just had to conjure up two more, didn't they, just to prove how creative they are! Well, we feel it's high time that 29 got its due, and not just because it's the age both of our wives are (and have been for several years).

Below, as a service to high-school seniors who don't attend BBC, is an extra-divine 29. The best of the best, if you will. (And we trust that you will.) It was heart-wrenching to cull the very wisest pieces from years of speeches. It was with great grief that we left advice like "Never spit in a woman's face—unless her mustache is on fire" on the cutting-room floor.

And now, with only a little dab of ado, here it is, the crème de la crème, the Dom DeLuise. The Hafer Brothers' All-Time Divine 29 Nuggets o' Wisdom for High-School Grads and Dreamers of All Ages:

1. Don't get too wrapped up in yourself; that's not a good look for you.
2. When you're tempted to criticize someone and you hold your tongue, chances are you won't regret it later. When you have the urge to say something kind to someone and you hold your tongue, chances are you *will* regret it later.
3. The next time you spend twenty minutes surfing 158 channels and still can't find anything worth watching, think about how much of your life you should invest in watching TV.
4. The future isn't in the stock market, high technology, or alternative energy. The future is in you and the abilities God has given you.
5. Don't work too hard at being a nonconformist. Those nonconformists are all alike.

6. When you enter a serious romantic relationship, don't lug a bunch of emotional baggage with you. Limit yourself to a couple of small carry-on items, at most.

7. Don't view the term "foolproof" as a personal challenge.

8. You're embarrassed about saying "I love you" now? Don't be. Or in fifty years you will be embarrassed about not saying those words nearly enough.

9. Respect won't necessarily come to you as you age. Respect should be earned through honesty and hard work. The same goes for money.

10. A clear conscience makes a great pillow.

11. Artificial intelligence is no match for good old 100-percent natural stupidity.

12. Blessed are you if you can laugh at yourself, for you shall never cease to be amused.

13. Don't be overwhelmed by the despair of a single moment or event. Just because you can't see hope doesn't mean it's not waiting to shine on you.

14. Always remember to say thank you.

15. If you find a true friend in this world, hold on for dear life.

16. Follow the best advice Elvis ever issued: Don't be cruel.

17. There's a reason the Golden Rule is called "Golden." Live by it, and you'll see what we mean.

18. Remember, only you can prevent narcissism.

19. Stay hungry.

20. Success in life isn't just about where you're

going; it's also about who you have beside you on the trip.

21. Be bold in what you stand for, careful of what you fall for.

22. Receiving accolades is a lot like smoking a cigar—it won't hurt you if you don't inhale.

23. Even a poor man can leave his family a rich inheritance.

24. You'll get lost in thought only so long as it's unfamiliar territory to you.

25. The world is a beautiful, dangerous place. Act accordingly.

26. Courage is simply fear that has said its prayers.

27. Never squander an opportunity to just shut up and listen.

28. Adversity in your life will demonstrate one of two things—what you're made of, or what you're full of.

29. Life is a journey, and no, we're not "there" yet.

ELVIS IS THE KING?
WHAT A HUNKA-HUNKA BALONEY!

Our town boasts many churches, from Southern Baptist to Eastern Mysticism. (One of our favorites—and this is a real one—is Saint John the Baptist Catholic Church. It's fun to hang outside this place on a Sunday morning; you always see a few flustered folks entering and exiting the building—sometimes within the same minute.) A couple of weeks ago a befuddled Baptist accosted us outside SJTBCC's doors. "Hey, am I too late to go in there?" he asked.

"Yeah," Jedd chuckled, "some would say about six hundred years too late."

Recently, however, a new church came to town, in a manner of speaking, and it's challenging SJTBCC for the title of Most Talked About Religious Institution. It's the Church of Elvis. This church has no building—perhaps because "Elvis has left the building." But he's "found a new place to dwell": in cyberspace. That's right; the Church of Elvis has broken virtual ground on that famous Al Gore creation, the Internet.

Please understand, we love the Internet. It's a great tool. But, like an electric cheese grater, it's a tool that's dangerous in the wrong hands. We know a few people who live their (so-called) lives online. You probably know people like this, too—more than you might imagine. After all, who wants to go around confessing, "I don't have any real friends or a life to speak of"?

The Internet is more than just a time waster, though. Its most frightening characteristic is that it allows diverse pockets of weird people to meet one another and form large clusters of cyber-winkies. This is not natural. These people were spread out across the globe for a reason. They weren't meant to coalesce. That's why God put New York and California on separate coasts and left a nice chunk of buffer zone—which the folks on the coasts affectionately call Flyover Territory—in between.

But now the Internet has allowed strangers from the Left Coast and the Far-Left Coast—as well as the Deep South—to join together and form the Church of Elvis. And these people don't just think Elvis was a neato guy. They adore him. They revere him. They seem to want to deify him.

The COE is a growing church, and we fear that even a few of our local residents are saying "Graceland" instead of grace. Lately we've seen sideburns getting longer and fuller. (And this wouldn't be quite so frightening if it were limited to men.) We know at least two women who have named their pets (one cat and one gerbil) Priscilla. And the other day Wilfred, one of our own church elders, complained that his wool sweater had him "itchin' like a man in a fuzzy tree."

Only in America would this happen. Sure, they love Jerry Lewis in France, but we haven't seen any ads for the Church of "Hey, Lady!" (And besides, at least Jerry Lewis has never worn shimmering jumpsuits that fit him like a coat of glossy latex paint.)

At this point, we should note that we have nothing against Elvis the Entertainer. We admire his talent and originality—and the way he bought cars for total strangers. We just don't like people calling him The King and refusing to accept the fact that he's dead. And if he were alive, we think he'd say, "What? Y'all built a church around me?! And the newspapers said *I* was weird!"

Let's be blunt: Jesus died on the cross. Elvis died on the toilet.

Don't Elvis worshippers realize what folly it is to form a church in his name? Let's be blunt here. Jesus died on the cross. Elvis died on the toilet. Christians wear crosses to honor their King. What are these "Elvistians" going to wear around their necks? Tiny commodes?

Christians also wear WWJD items to remind them to ask What Would Jesus Do? in a given situation. We're sure that it won't be long before we see WWED bracelets, T-shirts, bibs, and such. That way, Elvistians can be reminded to look to their role model when facing a dilemma.

In the spirit of freedom of religion, we'd like to help

Elvistians answer the question WWED.

Let's see . . .

> What would Elvis do? Eat a bucket o' fried chicken until he passed out.
> What would Elvis do? Shoot a TV set.
> What would Elvis do? Comb the peanut butter out of his sideburns and take a nap.
> What would Elvis do? Lots and lots of drugs.
> What would Elvis do? Sweat profusely.
> What would Elvis do? Really bad movies.
> What would Elvis do? Die on a toilet.

If you suspect any of your friends or relatives are converting to Elvistianity, please show them this chapter. Maybe you can show them the error of their ways. And if any members of the Church of Elvis are reading this right now, please let us say two things to you:

1. Wow, we're really surprised you can read!
2. You are free to worship whomever you wish, but please don't advertise your misplaced devotion on the World Wide Web. It's tangled enough as it is. We urge you to log off and consider who the real King is. We don't mean to be cruel, step on any blue suede shoes, or get you all shook up. We just want to straighten out this King thing. We appreciate your thoughtful attention. Thank you— thank you very much!

The Smashed Secretary

Our church was always the first phone number on the local law enforcement agencies' list of places to call when a vagrant was picked up in town. Our dad was also the first individual citizen on the list. Thus, we were guaranteed to meet every drifter who happened through our little village.

"I don't know why your dad sees the need to help all those vagrants," a friend's mother complained to us Hafer brothers one day. "Those bums—they aren't even human."

Our brother Chadd shrugged. "Our dad says that maybe if people will start treating 'those vagrants' like human beings, they'll start acting accordingly."

Dad's theory proved right. Not only were most of the folks he helped good-hearted and kind, they often blessed our lives while asking for very little, save some understanding.

Dad has a gift for being accepting. He was never shocked or repelled by drifters, even the ones who looked like they walked right off an episode of *Cops*—and smelled like turkey ranchers. He never recoiled, judged, or refused to offer help, even when onlookers felt he was being "taken for a sucker."

Don't get us wrong: There were times when Pastor Hafer was approached by individuals whose intentions were less than honorable. Fortunately, he also had a remarkable ability to tell the difference between legitimate need and illegitimate greed.

One Monday a kindly looking gentleman in a tattered jogging suit showed up at Dad's office at the church, seeking money. The man claimed he hadn't eaten in two days, but Dad was able to ascertain that he had consumed some fermented grapes and grain—quite recently.

Wisely, Dad offered to take the man to one of his favorite burger joints, the Dash-In: "It's just down the road, and I'll buy you a cheeseburger as big as your head."

"Oh, that's very kind of you, kind sir, and I do [urp] appreciate it," the man replied. "But it would work so much better for me if I could kindly just get the money for my own . . . uh, cheeseburger. Thank-ya-kindly!"

Dad raised his eyebrows in mock surprise, "You're going to turn down food after going two days without eating?!"

The man (we would later learn his name was Jeremiah) knew he was busted. He didn't argue, just put his head down and trudged off, presumably to try mooching off the Methodists or fleecing the Friends.

Dad left the office for the day and thought nothing more of it. He did not notice that Jeremiah had wedged a stick in one of the side doors, preventing it from locking.

After finding other sources for "food," the cagey Jeremiah made his way back to our church to crash in Dad's office for the night.

To Jeremiah's delight, the church secretary took the next day off and Dad spent it visiting people at the nursing home and hospital. That meant that Jeremiah had the run of the whole church. He went to the kitchen and prepared himself a couple of lightly toasted bagels. (This was an appropriate breakfast for Jeremiah, as he was also "lightly toasted.")

Around midmorning, a church member called to check on the status of the upcoming pancake breakfast. An unfamiliar, slurring voice answered the phone. "Buffylow, uh, Baptist Church, Jesus luffz yooo . . . erp, brother!"

Not amused, Mrs. Simms cleared her throat on the other end of the line. "Ahem. I am not your brother! Now, is this one of those awful Hafer boys pulling another prank?"

"Pastor . . . uh, big guy has employed me as a temporary employee in his . . . employ. How may I [hiccup] help you?"

"Oh no, ma'am," Jeremiah replied reverently. "Pastor . . . uh, big guy has employed me as a temporary employee in his . . . employ. How may I [hiccup] help you?"

"Well," Mrs. Simms' skepticism was still evident, "I'm trying to get a count for the pancake breakfast on Saturday. I'm in charge of bacon."

"Bless you, sister! I love bacon! I think we'll need a whole lot of bacon—I'm hungr ... I ... I'm sure there will be hungry ... I have a hankerin' there will be hunks ... I have a hunch there will be hunkerin' ... we'll need lots."

"Well, this is just an outrage! That's no kind of answer. You, sir, are not the least bit amusing. Tell Pastor Hafer I am not in favor of such tomfoolery!" and she hung up with much religious fervor.

The morning continued in much the same way. Many parishioners thought Jeremiah was putting them on; many more were upset by his antics. Our poor mom began getting calls at home around lunchtime.

"Your husband is drinking again!" cried Mabel Smigdel. (Helpful Explanation: We had never been able to convince Mabel that it was a mere misunderstanding when she called once during dinner as Dad was pounding on a stubborn bottle of Heinz ketchup. Chadd had answered Mabel's call and told her, "He can't talk right now—he's hitting the bottle.")

Mom calmed down the agitated Mabel and then called the nursing home to find Dad. He raced to his office to find Jeremiah snoozing behind his desk, feet up, snoring away contently.

We were proud of Dad. Most people would have been full of wrath—and he is a very big and imposing guy. But he simply woke Jeremiah up gently and then, after switching chairs with him, offered him a choice.

TODD & JEDD HAFER

"I have friends at the local hospital," Dad explained. "I'll call them, so they'll be expecting you. You can become a voluntary participant in an intensive detox program, or you can be admitted as an emergency-room patient."

Jeremiah shot Dad a puzzled look. "Emergency room? But I don't have any injuries."

Dad smiled, "No, not yet," he said evenly.

Jeremiah successfully completed the detox program. However, even if he hadn't, he was going to remain sober as long as he remained in Buffalo. Dad visited every liquor store owner and bartender in town, securing from each a promise not to sell to "the interim church secretary."

When he was released from the program, Jeremiah took Dad up on his cheeseburger offer. He also stayed around the church all summer, doing extra cleaning, fixing appliances in the kitchen, and making people smile. And every once in a while, after Dad checked his breath, Jeremiah even got to answer the phone.

Do You, Jedd, Take This Blame to Be With You Always?

Dad always warned us. He told us time and again that getting married, while being a wonderful gift from God, would change our lives forever. "To borrow a phrase from Mutual of Omaha's *Wild Kingdom*," he said solemnly, "you must learn to adapt, or perish."

Jedd was the most fortunate of the four Hafer brothers. He not only benefited from Dad's advice, but he was also able to watch his three older brothers take the plunge into Lake Matrimony.

"Marriage seems to agree with you guys," Jedd, then a high-school senior, told his siblings at a family gathering. "You dress better, you look happier, you bathe more regularly—and I keep getting free clothes every time your wives make you throw out the stuff they hate."

"Yeah, marriage is cool," Bradd said, "but there is something you should know."

Jedd's eyebrows arched. "What?" he asked.

Just then, three Hafer wives walked into the room. And the conversation ricocheted off in another direction:

Chadd: "That's a great idea, Bradd. We should turn off the football game and go clean up the kitchen."

Todd: "I concur. We certainly do watch too much football. It's not that important. It's only a game, you know."

Bradd: "Indeed. Let us now make haste to the kitchen. If we work efficiently, following our beautiful wives' examples, we should be able to finish before nightfall and get in an hour or two of yard work."

Chadd: "Then we can come back inside and have a Bible study with all the children."

So Jedd's question went unanswered. Days drifted by, and eventually he fell madly in love. He experienced the thrill his brothers had discovered before him—the fateful day when that special someone appears on your doorstep and you look through the peephole and exclaim, "Eureka! She's the most wondrous thing to grace my front porch since the pizza-delivery guy!"

Soon wedding bells tinkled, overjoyed relatives almost tinkled, and Jedd joined his brothers in the ranks of the married. That was a few years ago, and to this day, Jedd will tell you that his wife, Lindsey, is the pure joy of his life. (He'll be extra sure to tell you that if Lindsey is standing nearby at the time.)

Like his brothers, Jedd was soon dressing better, chewing with his mouth closed, and buying breakfast cereal based on fiber content, not on which toy was inside. All of these were changes for the better.

But, and here's the crux of Jedd's earlier unanswered question, he also began to realize that his station in life had changed. Because as soon as you accept the fact that you are now someone's husband, you must also begin to accept the fact that you are, suddenly and without warning, completely incompetent—and you now have someone to point that out every day for the rest of your life.

Other than just being there to make everything legal and all, the human groom at a wedding is about as important as the little plastic groom on top of the wedding cake.

Jedd's first clue as to his new life role came on the winds of the wedding ceremony. As was the case with his brothers, he wasn't consulted about any of the ceremonial details. His main job was to show up at the church on time. That's because, other than just being there to make everything legal and all, the human groom at a wedding is about as important as the little plastic groom on top of the wedding cake.

In fact, someday soon they won't even have little bride and groom figures atop the cake—they'll have a bride holding hands with HER MOM. That's right. Cake decorators everywhere will dispense with the pretense and start to showcase the two people who really matter. And if technology allows, these two figurines will be able to, with the push of a button, utter true-life wedding day sentiments, such as, "Boo-hoo-hoo! We should have gone with the teal napkins! Boo-hoo-hoo!"

Why this groomian insignificance? It's simple: Grooms are kept in the background on wedding days because their brides know that they will mess up everything if they try to get involved.

This tactic doesn't work for the rest of the marriage, however. Oh, the man is no more competent than he was on the wedding day, but now he can't just stand there in the frosting, trying to keep a low profile. Now he has to face the blame.

That's the key lesson Jedd has been learning since his wedding day. You see, people used to ask him for advice and guidance on a variety of topics, from lawn care to dog-obedience training. But since being married, he's discovered that he doesn't even know how to dress, groom, bathe, or feed himself properly. He also thought he knew how to drive. Ha! It turns out that he "doesn't know the first thing about piloting an automobile." And that's why he needs an expert driving instructor beside him at all times, critiquing his every turn, yield, and lane change. "Oh well," Jedd sighs sometimes, "at least she's a beautiful driving instructor."

It all comes down, as any of the Brothers Hafer will tell you, to blame. Before you are married, problems occur in the world and you feel no sense of responsibility or obligation toward them. But once you are married, you find that you can mess up things that you didn't even know about—and that you can get into serious trouble for things you don't say but look like you are thinking.

If you're having a hard time grasping this concept, it's probably because you're a married man, and therefore you're not very smart. A few years ago you would have understood it clearly. Not anymore.

So, to help you, here's Jedd with a real-life example of just how wrong and incompetent a married guy can be, without even trying. Read, learn, and apply it to your life.

"Recently my wife flew out of state to visit her family. I missed her very much, because she is the light of my life. (And I didn't write that just to earn brownie points by proclaiming my adoration forever in print—in a book that will be read by thousands of people.)

"Anyway, upon her return, I drove my car (carefully adhering to all traffic regulations) to the airport to pick her up. I found a spot in short-term parking and walked to the terminal to meet my beloved bride. After a warm but tasteful embrace, we headed for the parking lot. As I veered left, toward the car, which I parked, Lindsey said, 'You're going the wrong way. This isn't where the car is parked.'

"At this point, let's pause and review two key facts:

1. I, and I alone, parked the car.
2. While I parked the car, my wife was 30,000 feet in the air, asleep.

"Are you following this? She couldn't have known I was wrong. She could only assume I was wrong. But it wasn't assumption in her eyes. It was simple logic. It was a matter of instinct. I was wrong, because I was the guy and that's what guys do. We find ways to be wrong about stuff.

"That's basically the story. I guess I should add, parenthetically, as a minor footnote to this story that, uh,

I was wrong about where the car was parked.

"It took me twenty-five minutes to find the car. And, strange as it may sound, I found myself searching in lots in which I knew the car couldn't possibly be. It was like I was being magnetically drawn to the wrong spot. I felt my IQ dropping like WorldCom stock, and there was nothing I could do to stop it. I began to envy that little plastic groom.

"Truthfully, though, I wouldn't trade it all for any-thing. Considering how beautiful my wife makes life, I would never want to be a plastic groom—even if he does get to stand up to his ankles in delicious frosting and never has to drive or accept blame. You see, married life is way sweeter than cake frosting, and I'm sure I wouldn't get blamed for so many things if I'd be more open to correc-tion from my wise spouse. (And yes, she made me write that, but she was the one who ultimately had to find our car at the airport, so maybe she's right.)

"Or, just in case she reads this chapter: She's definitely right!"

The Wacky Morning Show Interview

Here's something we've learned about book publishing. Once a publisher decides to print and bind your book, then release it to the world at large, said publisher hopes that at least a few thousand people will buy the book.

Our publishers know that we will pester friends and relatives, who will buy a batch of books just to shut us up. And our former Web site, *www.twostarvingpreachers kids.com*, was a great sales tool until it caught a virus and had to be, in the words of our veterinarian pal Gregg Klanger, "put down like a scurvy-riddled kitty."

Finally, we'll garner a few more sales thanks to people with bad depth perception who reach for a LEFT BEHIND book and grab one of ours by mistake.

Unfortunately, the above don't generate the level of business needed to keep a literary work on store shelves and off of remainder racks (or bonfires). If you want your book to sell like hot cakes—or even Belgian waffles—you have to show that it's buzz-worthy. And if you're serious about the business of buzz, you must do media tours—

local TV, regional TV, UHF, local-access cable TV, whatever.

And let's not forget radio—lots and lots of radio. Radio is the staple of a successful book campaign. This means that we sit in a lot of stuffy radio studios, drink gallons of freeze-dried coffee, and converse with a variety of radio personalities. Some are funny; some are serious. Some are Christian; some are avowed atheists. Some have actually read our books; some haven't read a book since *See Spot Run*. And some, unfortunately, prove that sometimes "radio personality" is an oxymoron.

If you can't find one person with an engaging personality and sense of wit, fill the studio with half-, quarter-, or eighth-wits.

In many large cities, for example, the morning drive-time hours are filled by a team of wild and wacky characters, often called The Morning Zoo. We guess the strategy is that if you can't find one person with an engaging personality and sense of wit, fill the studio with half-, quarter, or eighth-wits and, perhaps by sheer volume of humanity, you'll jury-rig an entertaining show.

The following is a typical Hafer Brothers' visit to a Morning Zoo. (You'll note lots of sound effects in the interview. Why? Because in the event that three or four radio personalities can't be funny, it's nice to be able to fall back on the sound of a cow mooing petulantly.)

Host: Good morning to all my "dawgs" out there in the big city. This is Honkin' Hal, your radio pal! [goose-honking sound effect]

Punchy: What am I, Hal, chopped liver? Punchy is in "da house." Can I get some love? [sound effect of either two people kissing or a horse pulling its hoof from quicksand]

Lisa Love: Love? Did somebody say LUUUVVVVV?

Punchy: What's Love got to do with it?

Lisa Love: Oh, you're so bad, Punchy! [sheep-bleating sound effect]

Honkin' Hal: Hey, you two, cut it out.

Punchy: That's what my ex-wife said! [game-show-buzzer sound effect]

Lisa Love: Oh, Punchy, don't go there!

Punchy: She said that, too! [foghorn sound effect]

Honkin' Hal: Hey, are we wacky, or what?

Lisa Love: You da man, Hal. You said it! We are wacky!

Honkin' Hal: And speaking of wacky, we have two wacky dudes in the studio with us this morning. And later today, they plan to break the world teeter-totter record! My homeboys, what got you into teeter-tottering?

Jedd: Uh . . .

Lisa Love: Hal, you dingleberry, the teeter-totterers are tomorrow. Earth calling Hal! Earth calling Hal! Come in, Hal! [cat-yowl sound effect]

Honkin' Hal: Well, roll me in coconut and call me a tropical donut!

Punchy: Don't tempt me, my man. [cow-bell sound effect]

Honkin' Hal: Okay, so if you dudes can't teeter-totter, why are you here?

Todd: Well, we've written a book. . . .

Punchy: Cool beans! You know, I would like to write a book.

Lisa Love: Well, when it comes to being one wild and wacky dude, you sure wrote the book on that, Punchy! [sound effect of diesel engine revving]

Honkin' Hal: Hey, I wrote THAT book! I've been there, done that! I'm all that and a bag of chips! I've forgotten more about book writing than . . . than . . . uh . . .

Punchy: Than what?

Honkin' Hal: I guess I FORGOT! Isn't that ironic?

Lisa Love: I don't know; you better ask Alanis Morissette!

Lisa, Punchy, and Honkin' Hal: [hysterical laughter, followed by quacking-duck sound effect]

Jedd: Speaking of ironic, we—

Honkin' Hal: Sorry to cut you off, Jeff-a-rooski, but we are all outta time, my man. Thanks so much for being with us. I only wish our buddy Milo the Sad Clown wasn't out sick today. He would have loved you. You guys are great! They have been great, haven't they, Punch-man?

Punchy: Word up, Hal-dawg. We give you guys "dap" for chillin' with us this morning.

Todd: Dap?

Lisa Love: And be sure to buy their album, uh, what's it called, dudes?

Jedd: Actually, it's a book.

Honkin' Hal: Whatever! It's all good; it's all good, know what I'm sayin'? Again, fellas, thanks for getting up at 6 A.M. to help us get this wild 'n' wacky Wednesday started. Stay outta trouble, you knuckleheads! [police-siren sound effect]

Lisa Love: Be sure to stay tuned out there, listeners! After a break, Hal's gonna see if he can suck a quart of lime Jell-O through a bendy straw, using only his left nostril!

Punchy: Now, that's what I call good radio!

[If there were a sound effect for two brothers' hopes falling and crashing to the floor, it would happen right here.]

THE CONTENTIOUS CHRISTIAN RADIO INTERVIEW

Not all of our radio interviews are as wacky as the one in the previous chapter. And not all of them are on mainstream radio stations. Sometimes, in a show of Christian charity—or perhaps pity—a religious station will invite us to discuss our latest book. Most Christian radio hosts are congenial and positive, and their interview styles are gracious.

However, once in a while we encounter a host we can tell wants to be a religious Geraldo Rivera and grill us like a couple of burgers on the Fourth of July. Mr. or Ms. Contentious Christian Host is sure our book is fraught with theological errors and believes we need to be exposed for the shoddy, money-grubbing charlatans we are.

We endured an interview like this just last week (and we still have the grill marks to prove it):

> Host: Welcome back to *The Light of Truth* here on radio KILL. We're the program that shines the Light on folly, greed, and deception and makes evildoers scurry away in fear, like the despicable

cockroaches they are. I'm your host, Chris O'Contraire, and today we are talking to a pair of "Christian comedians," Todd and Jedd Hafer. Gentlemen, welcome to our show. Just let me know if the Light gets in your eyes and makes you uncomfortable.

Jedd: Thanks, Chris.

Chris: Excuse me, Jedd, but please call me "Mr. O'Contraire," "Sir," or "The Lord's Swordsman." Don't try to get familiar with me. We are not friends.

Jedd: My apologies, Sir.

Todd: I echo Jedd's apology. Please don't get sore at us, Mr. Swordsman.

If you'll treat me with the proper respect, I shall not unleash my wrath upon you.

Chris: If you'll treat me with the proper respect, I shall not unleash my wrath upon you. But let's get right to the point, gentlemen. According to your glossy press kit, which, I might add, looks very much "of the world" to me, you write humor books. This begs the question, Why? With all of the serious issues facing our world right now, is it really a time to be silly?

Jedd: Silly isn't really our goal. The Bible says there is a time to laugh and—

Chris: Hey, don't try to quote the Bible on me,

bucko! That's not going to work. I know the Bible inside and out, and I am not going to let you sit here and take verses out of context.

Todd: But, Sir Swordsman, that's not what Jedd is trying to do. All we are saying is that we are trying to bring much-needed laughter, in the spirit of Proverbs 17:22: "A cheerful heart is good medicine."

Chris: Oh, so you want to quote Scripture, too, huh, tough guy? Well, here's a verse for you: "I will send fire upon the house of Hazael that will consume the fortresses of Ben-Hadad. I will break down the gate of Damascus; I will destroy the king who is in the Valley of Aven. . . ."

Jedd: Yes, that certainly is a verse.

Chris: Indeed it is, and don't you forget it. But let's move on to something in your bio. It says here that you spent many of your formative years living in a trailer park. That makes you trailer trash, does it not? Admit it—you're just a couple of Jerry Springer–loving pieces of pagan white trailer trash, aren't you?!

Todd: Well, not exactly. Our dad always told us that we weren't trailer trash, because we lived in a double-wide, with skirtin'!

Jedd: Besides, we prefer the term "mobile home community" to "trailer park."

Chris: Mobile home, eh? Let me ask you something: Was your "home" truly mobile? Did you drive it around at night, looking for some den of iniquity in which to quaff sugary sodas and watch violent cartoons? Or is this whole mobile-home thing just another of your wicked lies?

Jedd: Well, Sir Sorehead—I mean, Sir Swordsman, our home wasn't mobile in the sense that we could drive it around. However, our roof blew off three times during windstorms, so in that sense, our abode was indeed mobile.

Chris: Ah, splitting semantical hairs with the sword of Damocles, are we?

Todd: Hey, we didn't touch Damocles' sword!

Jedd: Although we did borrow Demosthenes' butter knife once.

Todd (laughing): Butter knife! That was a good one, Jedd. I love a joke that involves tableware!

Chris: Forsooth from this tomfoolery! Can't you see that with each pathetic attempt at humor, you succeed only in losing face?

Jedd: That's okay with us. Over the years, we've lost more face than Michael Jackson. But we just keep trying.

Chris: Lost face? Michael Jackson? [twelve-second pause] Hey, I get it! Because of all his plastic surgeries, right? That was actually a pretty good line, Jedd. I don't know why I'm not laughing, though. Do you think, perhaps, I've lost my sense of humor somewhere along the way?

Todd: Well, it could be. Where did you use it last?

Chris: You know, I really can't recall. Do you think it's lost forever?

Jedd: I don't think so. I think you can find it if you go to a cartoon matinee this weekend. Check out that VeggieTales movie if you can. Go and sit in a theater full of laughing kids, and I think you'll find that the laughter is contagious.

Chris: By the beard of Obadiah, I'll do just that, Jedd!

I think it will feel good to laugh again. It's been too long. I guess the Light of Truth needs to lighten up. Hey, thanks, guys.

Todd: You are quite welcome, Mr. Sir Swordsman.

Chris: Please, call me Chris.

The Just-Plain-Cool Interview

Our favorite kind of radio interview is neither contentious nor wacky. What we enjoy most is when a host has (1) actually read our book, and (2) asks a question, then lets us run with it.

Hosts like this are wise enough to say to themselves, "Hey, my listeners hear me talk every day. If I'm going to go to the trouble of booking guests for my show, perhaps I should let them talk for a bit."

One of our favorite cool hosts is Rick "Rock-n-Roll" Radcliffe. He has a nifty alliterative name and a fast-paced interview style. (Also, he doesn't eat all of the jelly donuts in the Dunkin' Donuts box before we get to the studio.) Here's how things went the last time on his show, after we licked the jelly off our fingers and got down to business:

Rick: Welcome back to the show, guys. First of all, for those listeners who don't know you, please share a little bit about your background. Where did you grow up, and how did this color your writing?

Jedd: Well, we are still waiting to grow up. However,

we spent our youth in the wild, wild Mountain West of Colorado and Wyoming. This colored our writing beige, with green and gold flecks.

Rick: Were you good students in school?

Todd: Well, not "good" in the sense that we attended class regularly, obeyed all the rules, and earned straight A's. But in all of our years, neither Jedd nor I ever caused an accident or injury in woodshop.

Jedd: Mainly because we never took woodshop.

Rick: Of the classes you did take, which ones were the toughest?

Todd: Well, we hated history, because the teacher kept repeating himself.

Jedd: And don't forget about algebra. That teacher just had way too many problems.

Rick: Okay, enough about your teachers. Let's talk about your parents. Were they strict with you?

Jedd: Well, certainly more strict than we are with our own kids today. We had precise limits on how much TV we could watch. No more than an hour a night, unless a program with profound religious significance, like a Billy Graham crusade or a Denver Broncos game, was being televised. We haven't really enforced rules like that with our kids.

Todd: But maybe we should. I think my kids are watching too many of those police reality-TV shows. I knocked on my oldest son's door last night to see if I could come in and check his homework. He hollered through the door, "I don't know, Dad—do you have a warrant?"

Jedd: You know, we are trying to be enlightened, new-millennium parents, using positive reinforcement as much as possible and giving "time-outs" as punishment. But that wouldn't have worked for our dad.

Todd [chuckling]: Yeah, "time-out!" Ha! Back when we were kids, "time-out" meant how long we feared we'd be unconscious after Dad swatted us.

Jedd: And we were lucky. We didn't get punished nearly as much as our PK friend Dennis. His dad spanked him so much that he ended up with a severe case of Dennis Elbow.

Rick: Interesting. I see in your bios that music has played a big part in your lives. I hate to make you single someone out, but I want to know, for each of you, your number-one favorite recording artist.

Todd: That's a tough one, Rick. Hmmm, favorite recording artist? I'd have to say Richard Nixon. He did nice work.

Jedd: That's true, but Nixon's a little old school for me. I'll have to go with someone more contemporary: Linda Tripp.

Rick: Okay, let's try to get a straight answer outta you guys now. Let's talk books. Have any books been particularly influential on you?

Jedd: Well, I've been inspired by *True Integrity* by Jerry Springer. *You and Your Nostrils* by Dionne Warwick was also a good read.

I *am also enjoying the new cooking/self-help tome* Who Moved My Cheese Omelet?

Todd: I go for motivational books. One of my favorites is *You Can Play the Pan-Flute!* by Zamfir. I am also enjoying the new cooking/self-help tome *Who Moved My Cheese Omelet?*

Rick: Speaking of books, your work *Snickers From the Front Pew* raised a concern that I've been wanting to address with you. In that book, you say that your dog King actually came forward during an invitation at a church service. Is that true?

Todd: It's one hundred percent true.

Rick: Well, what was done with King after the invitation? Was there any follow-up? Was his decision taken seriously?

Jedd: Absolutely. We have a certified veterinarian on our elder board. After the service he took King to a nearby park for some lay counseling—and a game of fetch.

Rick: I see that our time is just about up, but I do have a couple more topics I want to get to. First, is it true that you write all your books out in longhand, in pencil?

Todd: Affirmative. We use pencil because we make so many mistakes. We don't know where we'd be without erasers.

Jedd: Since they are one of our sponsors, we should note on the air that we use Number 2 pencils exclusively.

Todd: That's right. Number 2 pencils—they're Number 1!

Rick: Well, what are you going to write next with those Number 2 pencils?

Jedd: Right now we're working on a book of free verse, which we're hoping we can sell for $29.95.

Todd: Our agent thinks we're crazy, though. He keeps telling us, "Free verse? You can't give that stuff away!"

Jedd: After that it's on to a couple of screenplays. The first is a horror movie with a canine theme. It will be titled *I Know What You Buried Last Summer*.

Todd: Then it's on to our Clint Eastwood western. Given his advancing age, we're thinking of going with the title *A Fistful of Geritol*.

Rick: Well, I hope both of those movies go places for you guys.

Todd: I'm sure they will go someplace. Straight to video, most likely.

Rick: Well, I see that I must go straight to the news. Thank you for being here today, guys. Any final thoughts?

Jedd: Yes, we would love your listeners' advice on some deep theological questions that have been troubling us. First, can you put self-tanning lotion on another person?

Todd: That one has kept us awake through many a church business meeting, let me tell you. As has this one: How do dragons ever blow out their birthday candles?

Rick: Intriguing questions, guys. I'll let you know if any listeners have insights for you. Where are you guys off to now? Any big appearances scheduled?

Todd: Not really. I'm just headed home to watch Jerry Springer. Today he will attempt to reunite one of his former guests with her dignity and self-respect. I'm dubious.

Jedd: And I will be continuing my counseling work with troubled houseflies—trying to help them get in touch with their inner maggots.

Small Dog at Large

(or, "The Dog Trial of the Century, Part 1")

*Greater love hath no man than that he goeth to jail
for his dog.*

—Rev. Del Hafer

During our childhood, the Hafer homestead served as
a refuge for myriad pets—from a pair of baby skunks
named Stinker and Pee-Wee to a rattlesnake named Eve.
(Yes, in naming our pets, sometimes we went for biblical
symbolism, other times for just plain cute.)

But in the Hafer Pet Pantheon, one of the all-time
favorites wasn't an exotic catch from the wild; he was a
fast little spaniel mix named Upchurch.

We selected the moniker Upchurch for two reasons:
First, to pay homage to Rick Upchurch, one of our favorite Denver Bronco players at the time. Second, when Dad
asked us, "Where did you find that mangy little mutt?" we
replied, "Up at the church."

Our parents agreed to let us keep the dog until we
found "a good home that really needs a dog." However,
even after a few announcements in the church bulletin

and two pleas from the pulpit, we could find no one who truly needed a scrawny stray mutt. When the phrase "dog pound" came up at dinner one night, the Hafer brothers almost resorted to tears. "Please let us keep him," Bradd pleaded. "He's small and won't take up much room."

"Besides," Chadd added, "he's great entertainment. He can catch a McNugget in mid-air!"

When Jedd promised that if we got to keep Upchurch we'd "never, ever sin again," our parents relented. They knew we had no chance of keeping Jedd's promise, but they thought if we could stay out of trouble for the rest of the week, it would be worth it.

Thus, Upchurch became "ours" one month after we brought him home. (In his canine mind, though, we suspect he knew he was ours three seconds after we found him at the church and gave him a piece of bubble gum—because that's the closest thing to food we had at the time.)

Like his gridiron namesake, Upchurch was lightning fast and nearly impossible to catch. We played a complex game called Chase the Dog with him nearly every day after school. He would snatch a battered purple Nerf football in his mouth, then dart and dodge through the yard as the four Hafer brothers tried to chase him down. We have relatively good speed—except for one brother we'll call "Jedd"—but we could catch Upchurch only if we cheated and called him over to us. (He fell for it every time.)

As weeks rolled by, we discovered another dimension to Upchurch's elusiveness. He was the Hound-Dog Hairy Houdini. Every night, when the spirited game of Chase the Dog was over, we would put Upchurch in the backyard, which was surrounded by a five-foot-high chain-link fence. The following morning we would find him sleeping on the front porch—or chasing the milk truck down the street with his neighborhood dog buddies.

So we built him a pen in the backyard, a pen with a roof and a lockable door. But within a few days Upchurch had tunneled his way under the pen, so he was free to leap over the fence and knock over a few garbage cans before breakfast.

In a large city, Upchurch's antics would have been a problem. But we lived on the outskirts of a town of 3,100 (2,800 with the wind chill), where leash laws were about as relevant as N'Sync lyrics. (Just a quick sidebar here: We don't want to anger our preteen readers by dissing a favorite boy band. It's just that to us, N'Sync isn't a group, it's where you put the dirty dishes.)

So we never worried about Upchurch. He never went far, he played well with other dogs, and he was always home for supper. Our mom, however, was concerned. "What if he gets picked up and taken to the pound?" she asked one day. "Are you boys going to cough up the money to bail him out? Because your dad and I won't."

"Aw, Mom," Jedd replied, "they'll never catch Upchurch. He's too quick, and he's too smart for them. Besides, the dog catcher hardly ever comes to our neighborhood."

Unfortunately, one quiet morning Mortimer Cane, the local Code Enforcement Officer (that's fancy city-government talk for "Town Dog Catcher"), did come stalking through our streets in his ominous seafoam green station wagon with fake wood paneling.

Morty hated to be referred to as "dog catcher." As a result, our brother Chadd called him just that every chance he got.

"Hey, Morty. Cool new dog-catcher suit," Chadd offered politely as the wagon stopped in front of our house.

"This," Mortimer hissed, "is the uniform of a City Code Enforcement Officer, and you will respect the authority of said uniform, got it, bucko?"

"Yes, sir, Officer Cane." Chadd smiled. "You catch any big dogs lately?"

"I enforce the codes of this community, you little reprobate," Morty said in his best Clint Eastwood voice. "Catching dogs is just one aspect of a comprehensive animal-containment program. By the way, I hear you have a new dog. You better keep him on a leash. If I find him to be, as we say in my profession, 'at large,' I'm haulin' him downtown."

At this point, we all made the mistake of laughing hysterically at the thought of Morty chasing our speedster pup. Even Upchurch, who was sitting on the front lawn gnawing his Nerf, seemed to stop and chuckle.

"What? You don't think I can catch that little mongrel? Just you watch me!"

With that, Morty jumped from his Pound-Mobile and dove for Upchurch's hind legs.

The chase that ensued was funnier than any Three Stooges/Keystone Cops/Laurel & Hardy movie we had seen. There was barking, growling, panting, snorting, and

gnashing of teeth. And the dog occasionally made a noise, as well.

Upchurch was loving the game. With Nerf firmly clutched in his jaws, he joyfully sprinted back and forth across our lawn, dodging and leaping whenever Morty came near. He racked up nearly two hundred rushing yards, without being tackled once. His tail was wagging, and his eyes sparkled with enthusiasm. He often looked over his shoulder at Officer Cane as if to say, "Good try, buddy! You're getting better at this, really. Keep it up! Let's keep playing!"

After a headfirst dive netted him only two handfuls of air, Officer Cane rose slowly to his feet. Exhausted and humiliated, he brushed a sizable portion of our front lawn from his uniform and walked slowly to his vehicle. As he departed, we noticed that he had ripped the seat of his Control Officer pants.

He often looked over his shoulder at Officer Cane as if to say, "Good try, buddy! You're getting better at this, really. Keep it up! Let's keep playing!"

Chadd, who still believed the whole incident was an exercise in harmless fun, called out, "Hey, Morty, you calling for backup? Hey, I respect your uniform, but I REALLY respect those Tweety Bird boxer shorts you're wearing!"

Officer Cane didn't reply, but he shot Chadd a look so sharp that it could have drawn blood.

In the days that followed, we learned of the vendetta behind that look. Yes, Officer Cane was out for vengeance.

From time to time we'd notice him parked across the street from our house, studying our games of Chase the Dog. He watched us intently, pausing sometimes to scribble notes on a clipboard. We feared he was scouting Upchurch's moves, looking for a weakness.

He found one.

Our dad happened to be looking through the curtains of our front window when Morty took Upchurch downtown. The officer didn't even have to stop his van. He just opened the window and called cheerfully, "Here, Upchurch," and our dog eagerly bounded into custody without a struggle.

The wagon was gone before Dad could get outside. (He had been watching *The People's Court*, which he prefers to enjoy in his underwear.)

Twenty minutes later, Mom and Dad led their four tearful children into the dog pound. "I hope some bulldog hasn't gotten Upchurch hooked on cigarettes and moonshine," Jedd sobbed.

Our tears must have worked—or maybe it was Mom's offer to bake Morty a pie—but Upchurch was released into our custody with only a warning. (Or, as Morty referred to it, "a slap on the paw.")

But three days later, Upchurch added to our city's sad dog-recidivism rate. In his zeal to chase down a squirrel, our dog cleared the back fence like a low hurdle and chased his rodent prey to the Burger King parking lot. As fate would have it, Officer Cane was exiting Burger King with Croissan'wich in hand as Upchurch chased the squirrel up a telephone pole.

This time, the system would display no leniency toward Upchurch. He received an official ticket for being "at large." Our dad was named codefendant on the ticket, which ignited his wrath. "Do you know how hard it is for a pastor to stay employed once he has a 'rap sheet'?" he complained over dinner that night. "I'm gonna fight this thing. This is just one more example of 'The Man' trying to persecute common folk. And what of poor Upchurch? Who will speak for him? We must go to court and defend his honor!"

We Hafer kids were delighted at the thought of a court battle. We didn't get to see crimson-faced grown-ups screaming at each other, except during church-league basketball season. And we were thrilled with Dad's passion for sticking up for our beloved dog. (Although we would learn later that Dad's primary motivation was avoiding the $20 dog-at-large fine because, as usual, we were about 30 cents short of a quarter.)

As Upchurch's day in Doggie Court drew near, we worked feverishly preparing his defense. Jedd posited the theory that the squirrel was in cahoots with Officer Morty and therefore this was a clear case of entrapment. "I can't stand it when a squirrel turns out to be a rat," Jedd said, pounding his fist into his palm. "He ought to be hung by his bushy tail for this!"

Unfortunately, in the final week before the trial, our self-righteous fire began to dim. The Hafer boys became occupied with Little League football and, occasionally, studying for a test in school.

Meanwhile, Dad and a few of the church's burliest men began training for the Annual Multi-congregational Interdoctrinary Tug-of-War. (That's "Tug-o'-War" for you Southern Baptists.) We were six-time champions, and Dad was the all-important anchor man for our church. Mom occasionally asked, "Are you guys going to be ready for Upchurch's trial?"

We always answered affirmatively, but our minds were preoccupied. She could have said something tragic, like "Oh, goodness, it says here in the paper that World War III has begun!" or "ESPN has been sold to a Swiss firm and it will now broadcast only yodeling tournaments," and we would have nodded and muttered, "That's swell."

Thus, on a cool September afternoon, the Hafer family, including Upchurch, went to the city park to try to outpull the Presbyterians, outmuscle the Methodists, and outtug the Trinity Lutherans. We completely forgot about the Dog Trial of the Century. But, as you can read in the next chapter, the trial didn't forget about us.

TO ERR IS HUMAN, TO FORGIVE, CANINE
(OR, "THE DOG TRIAL OF THE CENTURY, PART 2")

We arrived home from the Interdoctrinary Tug-of-War, victorious. Dad's grueling regimen of weight lifting and donut consumption had again made him the town's supreme anchor man. Dad's strength allowed two of our Tug Team's members to switch places in the finals, when Chuck the Elder complained that Gator the Youth Pastor's mullet was distracting him.

We all went to bed happy that night.

In the morning, the police came to our house to arrest the Reverend Hafer.

Dad opened the door to greet the two sheepish officers. "Hi, guys," he said cheerfully. "Would you like to come in and have a waffle?"

"Uh, no thanks," Officer Brett said. "Uh, that was a great sermon Sunday. It really blessed me. Oh yeah, and, uh . . . we're here to arrest ya."

Dad chuckled. "Okay, guys, which one of my sons put you up to this?"

Officer Brett wagged his head sadly and explained that

it was no joke. They said they would try to keep things on the QT but they had to take Dad down to the station ASAP to be booked on a warrant for an FTA (Failure to Appear) on a DAL (Dog at Large). There was no way around it. In a gesture of kindness, they let him finish his waffles and a BLT first.

They had to take Dad down to the station ASAP to be booked on a warrant for an FTA (Failure to Appear) on a DAL (Dog at Large).

As a matter of procedure, the officers had to handcuff our dad. Fortunately, they didn't bring their jumbo-size cuffs. And the conventional shackles wouldn't fit Dad's wrists, which are roughly the size of telephone poles. Being a good sport, Dad agreed to walk with his hands behind his back to make the whole thing look convincing.

We followed Dad and the policemen down our driveway, Chadd trying to add some levity to the situation by singing that "Bad boys, bad boys . . ." song from the *Cops* TV show.

Once Dad was secured in the back of the cruiser, Officer Brett slid into the driver's seat and turned the key in the ignition. The engine failed to turn over. The only sound was a brisk clicking from under the hood, akin to the sound a playing card makes when clipped to bicycle spokes. "Oh no," cried Officer Brant, Officer Brett's partner, "see what happens when you mess with a man of the cloth? The Lord hath struck our battery dead!"

Dad told the officers not to worry. Then he cheerfully climbed from the cruiser, drove our '72 Chrysler Newport into position, and gave the men in blue a jump start so that they could transport him to the station.

Mom was not as calm. She jogged after the cruiser as it backed out of our driveway. "Do you know that every ten seconds, a violent crime is committed in this country?" she yelled. "Shouldn't you be doing something about that instead of arresting one of the seven most upstanding men in the county? And furthermore, you made me scorch an entire batch of waffles, you tyrants!"

In the backseat, Dad just smiled. "One of the seven most upstanding men in the whole county! Wow—did you guys hear that?" he said proudly.

Then he poked his head out the window. "Thanks for saying that, honey. And I think you're pretty upstanding yourself! Save me some waffles, okay? I love you!"

At the police station, everyone seemed to be embarrassed over the whole DAL fiasco. Officers Brett and Brant turned Dad over to Ollie the Clerk for fingerprinting. Ollie loved Dad because several years earlier, Dad had performed Ollie's wedding ceremony. (Ollie and Molly, his wife-to-be, had wanted to be married while sitting atop their beloved horse, Thunderbolt. Five pastors in town said "Neigh!" to Ollie's request, but Dad said yes in a hoofbeat. He wore a Stetson and held his Bible in one hand and Thunderbolt's reins in the other as he conducted the ceremony in a field of alfalfa.)

"Pastor!" Ollie cried with delight before realizing why the renegade reverend was at his place of employment.

"Please tell your wife we enjoyed the pie she sent over to us when Molly was sick. And Thunderbolt enjoyed the carrots from your garden, as well. Uh, and please tell me you're not here under arrest!"

"It's true," Dad admitted as the rest of our family entered the station just moments behind him. "They caught me for something pretty awful. Rather not discuss it in front of my family."

Then Dad winked at us and shook his head. "I'm going down, Ollie. I'm going away for a long, long time—and I deserve it."

"Not you, Pastor! Why, you're one of the five most upstandin' men in this county!"

Dad shot a smug glance at Mom and held up five fingers triumphantly. "Top five on his list," he whispered. "Better move me up on yours."

"Pastor," Ollie pleaded, "this must be a mistake. I've never seen you hurt a fly. You're even careful not to squash a fella's fingers when you shake hands with those big mitts of yours. What could you possibly have done?"

"They got me on a Dog at Large rap, Ollie. Do you know a good lawyer?"

"They got me." Dad sighed. "They got me on a Dog at Large rap, Ollie. Do you know a good lawyer?"

Ollie cupped his face between his hands. "What in the Wide World of Sports!" he cried. "Why, I ought to tan your hide for scaring me like that, Pastor! But first I'm going to tan that fool Morty's hide! A DAL? Why, that no good . . . Just who does he think he . . . I'm going to . . ."

We realized that Ollie kept trailing off to avoid saying something unsavory in front of the pastor's wife and kids.

Dad was released on his own recognizance but was required to appear in front of Judge Jackson Gutterfield the following day.

Members of the community often sat in on Judge Gutterfield's court proceedings, for pure entertainment. "Judge Gutt" puts all of those TV adjudicators to shame with his charisma, similes, and simple witticisms. He's like Mark Twain in a black robe. And boy, can that man handle a gavel.

Court began with Ollie (who doubled as the bailiff) shouting ceremoniously, "Y'all rise!"

The Honorable Gutt waddled in, waving his hand as if swatting at flies. "Oh, sit down," he blustered. "All that ceremony in here is like having one of them fancy European Bee-days in an outhouse."

Dad snickered, being one of few in the courtroom who got Gutt's analogy.

"Pastor Hafer," the judge said, smiling good-naturedly, "let's hear your case first."

Dad stepped forward. "Good to see you, Your Honor. But I'm assuming that since you're the only judge in town, you must have signed my arrest warrant and you know why I'm here."

"Having two judges here would be one and a half too many," the great Gutt chuckled. "And I signed the warrant to get you in here. Haven't seen you at Mamie's House of

Pies lately. I miss our theological discussions."

"Sorry, Judge." Dad nodded. "I mean no disrespect to Mamie, but my wife's pies are so tasty that it seems unnecessary to eat much pie away from home."

With this, he glanced back at our mom, who was now indicating with her fingers that he had made it to the top three most upstanding men.

"Point taken," Judge Gutt said. "Now, as to the warrant, did you say the officers arrested you? They didn't just call and ask you to come in to court today?"

"It wasn't that bad, Judge," Dad answered. "At least not until they got out the nightsticks and pepper spray."

The judge was furious. "Why, those lunkheads! They don't have the sense God gave a goose! Chuzzlewits! If intelligence was cheese spread, they couldn't cover a single oyster cracker! Why, this is as outrageous as that John Davidson getting his own TV show a while back! You know, if I want to hear singin' that bad, I'll listen to myself in the shower!"

Dad nodded empathetically.

"Pastor Hafer, this is embarrassing." The judge's ears had turned stoplight red. "The only reason I wanted you to come was so I could return this to you."

He produced from under his bench a box containing Dad's power drill. "You loaned this contraption to me ages ago, and I've been meaning to get it back to you.

"You know, funny thing," Gutt continued, smiling at our mom. "You must take remarkable care of your tools, because it looks like you never even took this out of the box. You, sir, take that stewardship thing seriously, don't you?"

Dad grimaced, knowing he had now slipped back down into the seventh-most-upstanding spot. "I might have fixed or built something with it by now," he retorted. "It's been out of my hands since just after electricity was discovered."

Judge Gutt pounded his gavel and shook his head. "Good thing Ollie forgot to put you under oath, Pastor. You couldn't fix a leaky bottle of epoxy glue. That drill does you as much good as Morty the dog catcher does this city. Give me your ticket."

Dad complied. Judge Gutt examined the ticket contemptuously, then tore it into pieces and tossed them into the air like confetti. "I'll have no more of this nonsense today," he grumbled. With that, he tapped his gavel to the tune of "Shave and a Haircut" and declared, "Case closed."

Judge Gutt was lenient to us, but apparently canine-containment specialist Mortimer Cane didn't receive the same grace. We're not sure what Gutt said to him, but he came by the next day and apologized to the entire Hafer family, including Upchurch. He handed Upchurch a Milk-Bone and said, "I know we've had our differences, but let's bury the past and just move on, okay?"

Upchurch looked up at Officer Cane, then extended a paw of friendship and forgiveness. (After all, a dog in a pastor's family knows how to bury stuff, be it a soupbone or a grudge.)

In Search of Dad's New Tie

When we were kids, the scenario would play out nearly every Sunday morning: Our dad would be scouring the house for an article of clothing and eventually announce that he had "looked everywhere" and the item was nowhere to be found. Patiently, our mom would point out in her subtle way that if he had truly looked everywhere, he would have found it.

We were impressed by Mom's patience. There was no good reason that Dad couldn't find items in his wardrobe—especially during the 1970s, when many of Dad's multicolored polyester ties, shirts, and pants could actually be detected from outer space.

But Mom didn't scold him. She would just smile, reach into his closet, and produce the item in question. "Is this the green-and-orange striped tie with periwinkle giraffes along the border that you were looking for?"

"That's it! Where in the world did you find it?" he would exclaim.

"Oh, this strange, wonderful hiding place we like to

refer to as the closet—on what is known in some parts of the country as the 'tie rack'!"

"I looked there . . . twice," he would offer weakly.

"What, do you suppose, is the difference between your 'looking' and my 'looking'?" Mom would ask.

"Uh, men lack women's visual acuity?" Dad was lost.

"Men," she would lecture, "don't really look. The rods and cones of their eyes don't truly engage with the correct portion of the brain—known as 'the brain.' Women, on the other hand, really see things—like ties and messes and messy ties, crumbs on the counter, full garbage cans, towels and undershorts on the floor, clothes not matching—to the point of being offensive. You see, some combinations of clothing actually hurt our eyes, while you don't even notice."

We could pretend that Dad was the only can't-find-his-own-clothes culprit, but that would be dishonest (as well as deceptive and misleading). Beyond all that, it just wouldn't be true—so we won't make such claims (which, by the way, would be false). In the world of lost and missing clothing, we were as bad as Dad.

For example, our brother Chadd misplaced his wardrobe almost as often as Dad. And, like his father, he would complain to Mom that a given item had simply disappeared.

"Aren't those your boxer shorts on the dog?"

"Really," Mom would say. "Aren't those your dress

socks that your brothers are using to play flag football in the front yard?" Or, "Isn't that your Sunday school tie around your head as part of your pirate/commando outfit?" Or, "Aren't those your boxer shorts on the dog?"

Writing this chapter has made us appreciate the way that the moms of the world, and the wives of the world, keep their families organized, how their keen sense of observation saves their families from hours of fruitless searches—and from the expense of buying replacement clothes for those that are supposedly missing in action.

In fact, our sense of appreciation became so great that we wrote a tribute to the wives/moms of the world, the locators of lost loafers, the miners of misplaced mittens. It was a stirring tribute, and we know that scores of women would copy it from this book and place it proudly on their refrigerators. It would be made into plaques and wall hangings and quilts and key chains. Women would recite it at bridal showers and Bunko games.

Yes, it would touch so many lives . . . if only we could find it. It was written on either a napkin or the back of a church bulletin, and it was right here a minute ago. We'd ask our wives, but they are on a church retreat. They left us a number for where they are staying, but, well, that seems to be missing, too. Also, we aren't sure where the cordless phone is, anyway. Gosh, this is too bad, because that tribute really was meaningful. Hmm. I guess it's officially lost. Bummer.

At this point, all we can do is say this: Please appreciate the moms and wives of the world. Maybe when our better halves get home we can find the tribute, and we'll put it in our next book.

Bradd and Jedd Get Busted

Okay, it's Todd's turn to make the donut run, so this gives me (Jedd) the opportunity to tell you about yet another scintillating Hafer Brothers brush with the law. And this time there was no dog to help shoulder the blame.

I was ten years old at the time, six years junior to the second-youngest, Bradd. (And yes, I was "an accident." Thanks for wondering.) Both Bradd and I were too young to experience the harsh justice of the mean streets, but learn we did—and all because a well-intending family from our church "tithed" a motorcycle to our family.

Now, when I say "motorcycle," I mean a battered Kawahondazuki Deathtrap 250 Crosstrail dirt bike that was not exactly street legal. In fact, it was not remotely street legal.

So, naturally, Bradd and I decided to ride it through our small town to the church the first chance we got. It was a Friday afternoon. Dad was working at home, and he sent us for donuts and to his office to pick up the mail.

(Our family shared a P.O. box with the church, so the church secretary got the mail every day, then sorted the business stuff from our past-due cable TV bills, detention notices, and sports magazines, which she left on his desk.)

On this particular Friday we were particularly eager to see the mail, as we were awaiting delivery of a village of Sea Monkeys we had ordered from the back of a comic book.

Consumed with impatience, Bradd loaded his naïve younger brother onto the back of the Kawahondazuki Deathtrap 250 Crosstrail with exactly two functioning gauges, zero helmets, zero mirrors, and zero common sense. We took back alleyways during the one and a half miles to the church.

We were dismayed to learn that for the first time in recorded history, every single door to the building was locked. It was embarrassing—countless visitors, vagabonds, and stray cats had found their way into our church building with minimum effort, and here we were, stranded with no key, separated from our beloved Sea Monkeys.

We did the only sensible thing we could think of: Bradd climbed atop a trash can, and I climbed up on his shoulders to pry open Dad's window. (Our dad's office sat on the second floor, just off the sanctuary.)

I was just beginning to budge the dusty window when I heard a sickening, high-pitched moan. "Uh-oh," I thought, "I shouldn't be eating so many Nilla wafers every day after school. Poor Bradd has herniated himself."

But this noise was something even worse than what my added weight on Bradd's shoulders could induce. The local law enforcement "cruiser" had pulled up on the street behind us. "Hold it right there, wrongdoers!" we heard a voice shout.

It was one of Buffalo's finest, Bernie Pfeiffer, who never missed a trick (except when we super-glued the bottom of his left shoe to the floor of the Donut Shak. He was most upset because he didn't notice for nearly three hours.)

There he stood, nightstick in one hand, scowl on face, cheap sunglasses, the works, and we knew we were in trouble.

"Hey, Deputy Fife," I offered weakly. "Can you give us a hand with this window?"

"It's Pfeiffer, boys, with a PF, mind you. And I'll be giving you a hand downtown."

Apparently, "downtown" was his little nickname for the twelve-hundred-square-foot police station behind the Dairy Barn.

"This is not what you think! This is not what it looks like, Barney!" Bradd began to plead.

"That's Bernie! No, I mean Deputy Pfeiffer, you young hooligans! You yay-hoos may think you know me, but I don't know you."

"Sure you know us, sir," I gasped, climbing down from Bradd's shoulders. "You called us ne'er-do-wells after that unfortunate donut incident."

"And which unfortunate donut incident would that be, you ruffians?" Unfortunately, the deputy had been through numerous ignominious incidents at the Donut Shak. We blended in with all the other young "scamps and scoundrels" in the town.

Of course he knew of our dad, but he did not remember or believe that we were the pastor's sons. He hauled us all the way (four blocks) downtown in the cruiser (Chrysler station wagon with wood-grain siding and a crude star painted on the hood).

We were forced to sit in a small interrogation room where the conditions were frightening . . . well, it smelled funny and the vending machine was out of Zagnut bars. All attempts to call our parents were unsuccessful (Chadd was on the phone with some girl), and both of us had neglected to bring our stylish red Velcro wallets containing what Deputy P.F. Pfeiffer called "Verificatable ID."

No matter how much we begged, insisted, or filibustered, we were not released. Not until the kindly dispatcher lady returned from her dinner break and "verificated" that we were, in fact, Pastor Hafer's sons.

"These two ragamuffins?!" the deputy exclaimed in disbelief. "Are you sure? I know Pastor Del from the Donut Sha . . . I mean, we've discussed politics at length, and he always said his sons were good boys. These jackanapes are the fruit of his loins? I just don't see it!"

"You couldn't 'see it' if it was stuck to your ridiculous sunglasses, you *Starsky & Hutch* wannabe!" I muttered very softly under my breath as we walked from the station to return to the church. It would have been a louder mutter, but Bradd elbowed me and reminded me that we still had to drive home on the not-remotely-street-legal dirt bike.

So we had to wait until Saturday for our Sea Monkeys, and Dad had to get his own donuts. At the Donut Shak, he encountered our friend, Deputy Pf.

"Hey, Pastor, I met two of your sons yesterday."

"Impossible." Dad smiled to himself. "All my sons are away at a camp in Pennsylvania." (Our dad loves to tease law-enforcement people; he gets a charge out of poking a stick into the cage of Angry Fate.)

"Who were those delinquents I detained into the detention of my custody? Motorcycle hoodlums, I suspect!"

"I knew it!" howled the deputy as Dad turned to leave. "Who were those delinquents I detained into the detention of my custody? Motorcycle hoodlums, I suspect! By the burnished brass of my badge, I will find them and persecute them to the fullest extenuating circumstances of the law!"

At that point, Dad decided he had better 'fess up. Deputy Pf. was none too pleased with the joke, but Dad appeased him by promising him that we would name one of our Sea Monkeys after him.

And we made good on Dad's promise. We are pleased to report that Deputy Bernie the Sea Monkey thrived for a long time in a lovely fish bowl in the church office. We treated him with the utmost respect. We fed him lots of Sea Monkey Chow (and the occasional donut crumb) and changed his water regularly. But (and please don't tell the deputy this) we spelled the aquatic Bernie's last name Fifer! And sometimes we called him by his nickname, Barney. He never seemed to mind.

Parenting: More Than Diapers Will Change

In an earlier chapter we discussed how getting married changes a guy's life. But even matrimony, with all its waves of change, can't rock the boat of one's life like having children.

We will spare you the stuff about night feedings and burp cloths and singing purple dinosaurs. Other writers have expounded on these topics, so we see no need to reheat that particular microwave-safe bowl of beans-n-weenies at this time.

We want to focus on the biggest transformation that parenthood brings: The instant you become parents, you also suddenly become citizens.

Oh, sure, you're technically a citizen before. You have a driver's license, you think communism is a bad thing, and, if you have a sense of humor, you might even vote for a U.S. president once in a while.

Then comes a kid. And citizenship becomes a sure-enough priority. Forget the once-in-eight-years presidential voting stuff. Now you cast your ballot in every school board election, and you vote wisely, because you know each candidate's position on vital issues, as well as his or her employment history, blood type, favorite color, and favorite "Friend" from the TV show. ("You like Joey, and you think you can make school policy? Ha!")

You vote on every bond issue and every mill levy. (And before that, you take the time to learn what in the world those two terms actually mean.) You show up for town meetings on zoning, re-zoning, and re-re-zoning.

And that's only the beginning. You stop at every neighborhood Kool-Aid stand because you understand deep in your heart that it's your civic duty to do so:

> "Hi, Devin, I sure could use a Dixie cup of tepid Kool-Aid on a hot day like this. What flavor do you have there?"
> "Purple!"
> "Oh, goodie, that's my favorite!"

Moreover, to protect the safety of your own children—and that of young entrepreneurs like Devin—you begin to report potholes on nearby roads. And woe to the person who speeds through your neighborhood. Even if you are in your pajamas, you will run into the street to get the license plate number and perhaps to shake your fist and yell, "Slow down, you idiot. There are children around here!"

This child-induced citizenship is a good thing, for the most part. But it can create problems if it gets out of hand. That's what happened to Jedd a while ago, and that's why he can never call the police again.

Let us explain: A few evenings ago, Jedd heard

disturbing noises coming from the house next door. It was well after 9 P.M., which once you become a parent-citizen is "way too late for a bunch of noise and shenanigans to be going on!"

The noise in this case was that of the lady of the house, screaming at maximum lung capacity.

"Stop it!" she shrieked. "Get away! Don't kill me! Leave me alone! Don't kill me! Oh, please don't kill me!"

Jedd, a citizen with a parentally heightened sense of responsibility, scrambled for his phone and dialed 9-1-1. The police showed up and heard the screaming, too. They broke down the front door and were shocked to discover . . .

A mom and her eight-year-old little boy, playing a Nintendo game. She was screaming because her son was soundly defeating her by about 1,200 points!

Suffice to say that this mom won't ever lend the Jedd Hafer family a cup of sugar or anything else. And the police made it clear that they didn't want any more emergency calls from Casa de Hafer.

So even if a deranged, machete-wielding maniac shows up at Jedd's house, he can't call the police. "Oh yeah," the dispatcher would say sarcastically, "we better just hustle right over there. Could be another possible Donkey Kong in progress." Forget about the boy who cried "Wolf!" Jedd is the boy who cried "Super Mario!"

However, being a parent-citizen carries its benefits as well as its drawbacks. You see, before we had children, we had no problem being rude or downright caustic to telemarketers who called up at dinnertime, wondering if we'd like to turn our back on our current long-distance phone carrier and switch over to a completely new system, with new rules, requirements, and billing procedures, all for the sake of saving twelve cents. We also had no problem hanging up on these folks as soon as they'd say, "Hello, Mr. Haff— . . . Mr. Heff—. . . Mr. Hoffenhammer, are you happy with your current—?" [Insert resounding *click* here.]

But now that we're parents, we can't verbally abuse or rudely hang up on telemarketers. That wouldn't be good citizenship. It wouldn't set a good example for our children.

This creates a dilemma, though. Because while we don't want to be rude, we also don't want to buy a bunch of crud we don't need and can't afford. (Besides, we both tried "The Abdominizer" and we still don't have abs like Leonardo DiCaprio. Ours abs more closely resemble those of Leonardo DeNimoy-o.)

Thankfully, we discovered that the answer to the above dilemma was as plain as the tiny hands that are trying to pull the noses off our faces: That's right, our children. You see, as adults, we don't like talking on the phone to strangers. But our kids love it.

When Jedd's son Bryce turned two, he was designated Official Telemarketer Ambassador.

When Jedd's son Bryce turned two, he was designated Official Telemarketer Ambassador. Jedd would let a telemarketer start his spiel, then hand the phone to Bryce. The system worked like this:

> Telemarketer: So, Mr. Heffenmeyer, can I interest you in our money-saving blah blah blah . . . with no cash down and blah blah blah . . . no long-term obligation yammer yammer yammer . . .
>
> Jedd (covering mouthpiece with hand): Bryce, come talk on the phone. It's GRANDMA!
>
> Bryce (into phone): Hi! I go on potty like big boy! I got new Batman toy. I love SpongeBob Square-Pants! Do you love SpongeBob SquarePants? Wesley push me down at church! Wesley naughty. . . .

When your children get older, you can still employ them as telemarketer troubleshooters. Especially when they are old enough to have attended Girl Scout camp, like Todd's daughter, Jami.

So beware, telemarketers of the world, because when you call the Todd Hafer household, the only response you're going to get to your questions is Jami's rousing rendition of camp-time favorites like this:

> I KNOW A SONG THAT GETS ON EVERY-BODY'S NERVES! EVERYBODY'S NERVES! EVERYBODY'S NERVES! I KNOW A SONG THAT GETS ON EVERYBODY'S NERVES, AND IT GOES JUST LIKE THIS . . . I KNOW A SONG THAT GETS ON EVERYBODY'S NERVES . . . [ad infinitum, ad nauseam]

We know that some of you out there might criticize us for employing our children in this manner. But please understand, they love it. They often have trouble getting adults to listen to them, so the concept that total strangers are calling us on the phone, eager to chat, is a real thrill.

Besides, the effective handling of phone solicitors is a skill that any good citizen should learn. We are teaching this crucial skill to our children today so that they might delegate it to their own offspring someday. You see, with us, citizenship has become a family tradition. A legacy. And couldn't your household use a little more legacy, fellow citizen?

Things to Do During a Dull Sermon

We write this chapter at our own peril. We know that after reading it, our dad will start glaring at us in church as if to ask us, accusingly, "I'm not BORING you now, am I, you little reprobates?!"

That's okay. We can take the heat. Because, let's face it, folks, boredom blindsides even the most saintly parishioners once in a while. Some Sundays your blood sugar is too low or you didn't get enough sleep the night before. Or it could be that your pastor, like even the toughest baseball relief pitchers, doesn't have his "best stuff" some days.

Other times your church hosts a "special guest speaker" who turns out to be not all that special.

In cases like these, you have two choices.

1. You can pretend to pay attention. You can nod your head, as if you're agreeing with what the pastor is saying. You can rub your temples, as if you're trying to massage the message into your brain. You can stare at the pastor, as if you're transfixed by

both the medium and the message. But in all these cases, what you're really trying to do is simply stay awake while fooling others into thinking that you're so into the sermon that you can't possibly just sit there and listen like a normal person. Sure, this choice might seem polite, but is it honest?

2. Just admit to yourself—and demonstrate openly to others—"For whatever reason, I seem to be bored today. Rather than feign my spirituality and thereby attempt to deceive my beloved co-worshippers, I am going to find something to do while I wait for the sermon to end. Then I'll come back next week and hope I am more attentive. Please judge me not. Let him who is without occasional sermon-induced boredom cast the first X in a game of tic-tac-toe to be played on the back of my bulletin."

Rather than feign my spirituality and thereby attempt to deceive my beloved co-worshippers, I am going to find something to do while I wait for the sermon to end.

In case you find yourself a Bored Member in church some Sunday and decide to dispense with pretense, we've collected the following Preacher's Kid–Approved pastimes for those occasional dull days. Each of the activities below is non-obtrusive to people around you and should

keep you occupied for up to thirty minutes. (Sorry, if you end up bored at an all-day revival, you're on your own.)

The Hafer Brothers' Officially Sanctioned Activities for Passing the Time During a Dull Sermon
(Also Approved for Use in Cantatas, Business Meetings, and Church Elections)

1. Scan the congregation, person by person. Determine whom you could beat in arm wrestling, who would out-muscle you, and who would push you to a sweaty, biceps-cramping tie. Determine your overall record. If there is still time, do the same exercise, this time pitting yourself in a hypothetical Indian leg-wrestling match with each parishioner. (By the way, win or lose, remember to pray for each of your theoretical foes. It's the Christian thing to do.)

2. Page through your hymnal and see who wrote the most hymns. (Note: If your church is old school like ours, Fanny Crosby is going to be hard to beat. But John W. Peterson and Bill Gaither are going to be contenders, as well.) If your "hymn-off" comes down to a draw between two composers, the total number of stanzas or the number of times the word "o'er" is used can serve as tie breakers.

3. Create festive origami animals from the used Kleenexes in your wife's/mother's/grandma's purse. If you have time, create two of each animal, fold your bulletin into the shape of an ark, and march your critters inside.

4. Study people in your congregation for garments with a food theme. (This could include hats with fake fruit on them, ties dotted with loaves & fishes, VeggieTales T-shirts, or even a purse shaped like a meat loaf.) See how many items on the Food Pyramid you can find. (As a variation, commit to preparing your after-church meal only with foodstuffs represented on parishioners' clothing or accessories.)

5. Turn a few of your favorite Bible stories into limericks or another style of cute rhyme. For example:

- *The Good Samaritan*
  A poor man lay on the road
  Robbed and beaten and scared
  He thought he would die
  Till a kind passerby
  Helped and showed that he cared.
- *The Exodus*
  Pharaoh was so mean;
  He was such a fiend
  That God's people all had to flee
  They thought they'd get caught,
  But their God said, "not!"
  And made them a path through the sea!
- *Balaam's Donkey*
  Balaam had a donkey
  who always did what she was told
  until one day she saw an angel
  standing in the road.
  On that day that donkey stopped
  and wouldn't even budge,

so Balaam whacked her with a stick.
(It was more than just a nudge!)
The donkey said, "Stop hitting me!"
and Balaam's jaw just dropped.
But then he saw the angel, too,
and was glad his donkey stopped.

- *The Prodigal Son*
A young man did something quite bad
that made his poor dad very sad.
He ran far away,
but came back one day
and that made his sad dad quite glad!

6. If option No. 5 isn't hip enough for you, try turn-
   ing a Bible story into a rap. Here's an example, yo!

- *The Red Sea Rap*
Everybody listen up as we rock the mike,
Gonna tell you all a story that we hope you like,
'Bout God's people put in chains by the big
Pharaoh
Until Moses told him, "Homey, time to let 'em
all go!"
Now, God had said to Moses, "Yo, Mo, you da
man!"
And Moses had replied, "Who, me?"
God said, "Word up, Mo, 'cuz I have a plan
To set all of my people free!"
So Mo stepped to Pharaoh, all big and bold
And said, "Yo, my man, you better let them go!"
Go-ohhhhhhhhhhhhhh! Go-ohhhhhhhhhhhhhhh!

But Mo said, "God, it's no good—ya see I gave it
a try,
But that old Pharaoh just up and punched me in
the eye."
God said, "Sweat not," as he kicked the bass,
"Let's see how he likes some flies all up in his
face!"
Then the Lord kept on goin' when the Pharaoh
didn't quit.
God sent gnats, frogs, and hail—He was throwin'
a fit.
But that Egyptian stood stubborn with his hat
down low.
He crossed his royal arms, and he still said
"NO!"
No-ohhhhhhhhhhh! No-ohhhhhhhhhhhhh!

Next, Mo warned Pharaoh (after the locusts
were done),
"Wise up, or God's gonna take your firstborn
son."
So Pharoah learned too late: God's power's no
joke
And Moses, God's servant, wasn't blowin' no
smoke
But he finally agreed, with his hat down low,
"I've had enough, Mo, now will y'all PLEASE
go!"
Go-ohhhhhhh! Go-ohhhhh! Go-ohhhhhhhh!
    (big finish)

BETTER READ THAN MISLED

Hey, guess what? Bless you for reading this book! We're serious about this. And we're not just trying to ingratiate ourselves to you because without literate people like you in the world, we'd have to go to Radio Shack and beg for our old jobs back. You see, we worry a lot about our country and its future. We fear that the handwriting is on the wall, but too many people won't (or can't) even read it.

Too many of us would rather watch manufactured sitcom clans—with potty-mouthed kids and bumbling parents—than read about how to relate to our real-life families.

And we seem to relish the feeling of superiority we glean from watching a moronic audience cheer as two obese women try to strangle each other over a cheating boyfriend who owns even fewer brain cells than teeth. Compared to these folks, we're Mensa material, so why read a book that will make us think about important life issues or encourage us to better ourselves physically, mentally, socially, or spiritually?

Many Americans Just Say No to Knowledge. If it takes effort to learn about something, they'll pass. Why learn from Lewis, study Shakespeare, consider Colson, meditate on Manning, or devour Dostoyevsky when TV is serving up such fare as *World's Grisliest Animal Maulings; Survivor 8: The Planet Neptune;* or *The Bachelor 6: Alfie Marries a Mermaid?*

TV is much tidier than reading, too. There aren't those pesky pages to turn. With a book, you finish one spread and you have to flip to the next one. TV, on the other hand, is seamless. You don't have to do anything. And you're interrupted only once every nine minutes or so by scantily clad supermodels or washed-up actors who want to make your lives better through beer, lotion, and high-fiber cereal.

Want to do a little sociology experiment this week? Go to your local library on a Friday afternoon or evening. Then go to your local video store. Chances are, the video place will be packed, while the library will be as empty as a politician's promise.

Please understand us: we're not saying that TV is the great scourge of society. There are some creative, well-written shows, and these gems should not only be applauded but supported. One of the best ways to nurture excellence is to feed and water it when you see it sprouting.

Our concern is that TV's primary purpose is to entertain. It isn't designed to provide in-depth knowledge. Even the news—the part of TV that is meant to inform—is really just a collection of teasers, sound bites by famous people, and a few "on-the-spot reports" that feature a reporter standing outside a house saying something like, "Information is sketchy at this point, but what we do know is that something went on in the house behind me, and an alleged hyena was allegedly involved. Now, back to Murphee and Bunnee in the Eyewitness/Doppler 5/Super Satellite Studio for the conclusion of our six-part special feature, 'Oh, the Marvelous Yam!' "

At its best, TV is like gargling at the Fountain of Knowledge.

You can't learn much from a batch of itty-bitty bites, just as you can't gain nourishment from a hamburger merely by nibbling a few sesame seeds off the bun.

At its best, TV is like gargling at the Fountain of Knowledge. Books let you drink deeply. Books allow you to truly explore a subject—from a variety of angles and perspectives. And most authors aren't trying to sell you a bunch of products between chapters. For the most part, we trust you as to which laundry detergent to buy, and we'll like you just fine even if your teeth aren't dazzling white and your armpits don't smell like a pine forest. Moreover, how you deal with your various digestive woes really isn't our business, unless we happened to be trapped in an elevator with you.

Books can give you the knowledge you need to act

wisely, act fairly. Books, not a TV remote, are the keys to knowledge. Our future will be shaped by the readers and doers of this world. (And the readers and doers, in all likelihood, will have to carry the couch potatoes. When you do this, bend your knees and lift with your legs, not your back. We read that in a book.)

So again, thank you for reading. The ability to read, then think and act on what you've read, is a gift. Please share this gift whenever you get a chance, okay?